ADVANCE PRA[
UNLEASHED LEADERSHIP

We've partnered with Garland and Dorothy for years to develop leaders across Rollins and shape a People First culture. *Unleashed Leadership* offers a simple, clear, and practical roadmap to help leaders at all levels overcome what's holding them back—and impact the people they're leading.

—Jerry Gahlhoff, Jr.
Chief Executive Officer and President, Rollins, Inc.

I've read hundreds of leadership books and interviewed many of their authors—and *Unleashed Leadership* stands out. It delivers the kind of practical tools leaders can actually use, not just talk about. Garland and Dorothy have created something special here, and I can't wait to read the rest of the series.

—Jeff Brown
Coach, speaker, podcaster, and author of *Read to Lead: The Simple Habit That Expands Your Influence and Boosts Your Career*

We've used *Unleashed Leadership* throughout our manufacturing organization—from executives to plant managers to frontline supervisors. It offers leadership strategies that are grounded, usable, and built for the real demands of day-to-day operations. This book doesn't stay on the shelf. It shows up in conversations, decisions, and growth across the business.

—Jeffrey Smith
2x CEO of Manufacturing Organizations

If you want your business to grow, your leaders have to grow first. *Unleashed Leadership* makes that possible by helping leaders identify what's holding them back and giving them the tools to move forward. It's a smart, strategic approach to leadership development that every HR leader should pay attention to.

—Debra Martinez
Vice President, Human Resources, Global Operations,
Weatherford

Leadership shows up in every customer interaction and every team decision. *Unleashed Leadership* gives leaders the clarity and focus they need to grow their people and deliver consistent results. It's a powerful resource for anyone who wants to lead with both heart and excellence.

—JR Pasion
Chief Executive Officer, Bonney Services Holdings

Unleashed Leadership is ultimately a book about trust, trusting yourself, trusting others, and creating the kind of culture where people flourish. Garland and Dorothy Vance have given us more than leadership principles; they've given us a blueprint for rebuilding trust in a world where it's often broken. This book calls leaders back to authenticity, integrity, and consistency, the very foundations of trust. If you want to be a leader who is not only effective but also deeply trusted, *Unleashed Leadership* is your guide.

—Larry Levine
Author of *Selling from the Heart* & *Selling in a Post-Trusting World*, Co-host of the *Selling from the Heart* & *Culture from the Heart* Podcast

Leaders come in many forms. Each of us is divinely designed for success, created to thrive in our endeavors and to grow into the best version of ourselves. Unfortunately, the reality of daily life can disrupt that intended success if we are not adequately prepared. *Unleashed Leadership* is your guide to properly prepare to be the leader you were destined to be.

—**Scott Ferguson**
Multi-Family Manufacturing Market Manager,
Builders FirstSource

In today's world, leadership development isn't optional; it's essential. *Unleashed Leadership* offers a clear, practical pathway to help managers grow into the leaders their teams need. Garland and Dorothy have distilled years of experience into a framework that's both accessible and transformational. If you're serious about becoming a better leader, do yourself a favor and grab this book!

—**Ali Merchant**
Founder All-In Manager, Former Head of L&D (2X)

I've had *Unleashed Leadership's* seven traits taped to my desk for years—and for good reason. This framework has shaped how our leadership team at Orkin Canada approaches the daily challenges of leading people. Garland and Dorothy offer clear guidance to help leaders respond intentionally. It's practical, powerful, and deeply relevant.

—**Rob Quinn**
President, Orkin Canada

Throughout my career, I have seen top-performing companies invest in identifying and developing leaders to help the company achieve desired business results and to build a culture where their employees are happy and productive. Leading a team of people is hard, and it is not for everyone. I have witnessed leaders who were on a leash. Invariably, those leaders fail. *Unleashed Leadership* provides a very systematic approach to leadership development, both for leaders and companies. I love the 3 stages and the 7 traits outlined by Garland and Dorothy. They are simple and easy to follow. They are practical and make sense. This book will help organizations grow leadership strength at all levels. It is a must-read!

—Quentin Misenheimer
Chief People Officer, Garlock Flexibles (an Astara Capital Partners company)

Leadership is complex. It's never easy. But *Unleashed Leadership* makes it easier by helping you focus on the right things. Garland and Dorothy have created a clear and practical path for leaders who want to grow themselves and lead others with greater impact.

—Dusty Holcomb
Founder & CEO of The Arcqus Group

Every business leader needs *Unleashed Leadership*. It cuts through the noise and gets to the heart of what's holding leaders back. Garland and Dorothy don't just identify the problems— they show you how to build the traits that will unlock your greatest impact. Clear, actionable, and deeply insightful.

—Mike McLeod
Chief Executive Officer, Edge Energy Group

UNLEASHED LEADERSHIP^{IP}

How to Solve the 7 Issues
Holding You Back from
Your Greatest Impact

UNLEASHED LEADERSHIP

HOW TO SOLVE THE 7 ISSUES HOLDING YOU BACK FROM YOUR GREATEST IMPACT

Dr. Garland Vance

Dorothy Wood Vance

ethos
collective

Published by Igniting Souls
PO Box 43, Powell, OH 43065
IgnitingSouls.com

LCCN: 2025910235
Paperback ISBN: 978-1-63680-523-8
e-book ISBN: 978-1-63680-525-2

Available in paperback and e-book.

The Unleashed Leadership Series is
dedicated to our most important people:
Our parents, who led before us.
And our children, who lead behind us.

Table of Contents

Foreword by Kary Oberbrunner...13

Introduction...17

ORIENTATION

Chapter 1   How Leaders Become Leashed...........................25

Chapter 2   What Is the Leash?..27

Chapter 3   How We Became Unleashed..............................31

Chapter 4   Defining Leadership..39

Chapter 5   The Seven Leadership Issues of a Leashed
Leader..47

HOW TO GET UNLEASHED

STAGE 1: DECIDE...55

Chapter 6   Is Getting Unleashed Worth It?.........................59

Chapter 7   Decide How to Drive Your Strive 69

STAGE 2: DISCERN 75

Chapter 8   Name the Presenting Problems 79

Chapter 9   Identify the Underlying Leadership Issue(s)......83

Chapter 10 Determine Your Critical Actions........................93

STAGE 3: DELIVER 99

Chapter 11 Activate Your Critical Actions 101

Chapter 12 Accelerate Your Unleashing............................105

Conclusion 111

Garland's Thanks 121

Dorothy's Thanks...123

Our Thanks...127

About the Authors 131

Foreword
by Kary Oberbrunner

OVER THE PAST two decades, I've had the privilege of working with thousands of leaders and entrepreneurs—men and women with vision, grit, and talent. Many were leading teams, launching businesses, and building movements. From the outside, they looked strong. But behind closed doors, a different story often emerged.

They were exhausted. Frustrated. Confused.

They couldn't pinpoint the problem, but they knew something wasn't working. So they pushed harder, worked longer, tried to lead better. But the more they fought, the tighter the leash felt—like something unseen was holding them back.

If you're reading this, maybe that sounds familiar.

Throughout my career, I've had the opportunity to work alongside some of the greatest leadership minds of our time, including John Maxwell—who has shaped generations of leaders—and Dan Sullivan, the founder of Strategic Coach and the world's foremost entrepreneurial coach. I've seen what real leadership growth looks like. That's exactly what *Unleashed Leadership* offers.

It doesn't offer quick fixes or tired clichés. It offers deep transformation. It names the reality most leaders feel but few can articulate: *effort alone isn't enough.* You can't solve what you haven't diagnosed. And you can't grow past what you haven't named.

Garland and Dorothy introduce the seven root issues that covertly sabotage leadership: Character, Competence, Capacity, Clarity, Community, Culture, and Consistency. These aren't surface-level ideas—they're deep truths that explain why even great leaders get stuck.

The first time I saw this framework, I thought: *This is it.* It puts language to patterns I'd seen in myself and others. It gave me a way to help leaders move from stuck to strategic, from overwhelmed to overcoming.

Once you see the root issue undermining your leadership, everything changes. You stop chasing surface solutions and start solving the real problem. You no longer rely on sheer effort to carry you through. Instead of pulling harder on the leash, you finally start escaping it.

Unleashed Leadership is more than a book. It's a turning point.

So if you're tired of white-knuckling your way through leadership... if you're ready to trade exhaustion for effectiveness... then turn the page.

The shift you need is right here.

—Kary Oberbrunner
CEO and *Wall Street Journal* and *USA Today* Bestselling Author

THREE STAGES TO
UNLEASH YOUR LEADERSHIP

01 DECIDE

- [ ] Evaluate if you are currently leashed (Chapter 2)

- [ ] Determine if it's worth it to get unleashed (Chapter 6)

- [ ] Choose your striving method (Chapter 7)

02 DISCERN

- [ ] Name the presenting problem(s) you're currently experiencing. (Chapter 8)

- [ ] Identify the underlying leadership issue(s) causing those problems. (Chapter 9)
    1. Character
    2. Competence
    3. Capacity
    4. Clarity
    5. Community
    6. Culture
    7. Consistency

- [ ] Determine your critical actions. (Chapter 10)

03 DELIVER

- [ ] Activate your critical actions (Chapter 11)

- [ ] Accelerate your unleashing (Chapter 12)

Introduction

LARRY HAD JUST been promoted to Senior Manager of a service company that had over 20,000 employees. As he walked into his new office on his first day, he felt a mix of excitement and pride. He had worked hard and earned this.

His boss shook his hand, patted him on the back, and said, "We're counting on you."

It wasn't long before Larry was completely leashed.

Over the years, Larry had been repeatedly promoted because of his "everything is figure-outable" attitude. Ambitious, hard-working, and a problem solver, supervisors recognized him for his ability to thrive in any role, in any company. He set the pace for the office—the first to arrive and last to leave. It wasn't the work alone that Larry cared about; he also valued the people he worked with. Ensuring his teammates enjoyed their jobs became a personal mission. He frequently took responsibilities off their plates to ease their stress and lighten their loads.

On his first day in his new role, Larry sat down at his desk, opened his laptop, and saw 374 unread emails.

His new responsibilities hit him like the weight of collapsed scaffolding.

Over the next few weeks, Larry drowned in meetings, emails, and expectations. His inbox never stopped filling up, and his calendar had no empty space. The CEO delivered directives one day and changed them the next.

While Larry was used to being an equal on a team of peers, now everyone looked to him for answers. Every day, someone knocked on his office door.

"Larry, got a second?" meant 45 minutes of solving someone else's problem.

"Hey, just looping you in," meant an email chain with 15 people who all expected a response.

"What should we do about this?" meant they were waiting for him to decide.

At first, Larry tried to handle it all. He worked longer hours, took his laptop home, and answered emails at night. But no matter how much he did, it was never enough.

Then the cracks started to show.

Three months in, Larry lost his first employee—one of his best team members. She said she left for a "better opportunity," but her exit interview revealed the truth. She was frustrated with Larry. She said he lacked direction, wasn't available when she needed him, and that she didn't believe he was a good leader.[1]

The next blow came from above. Larry's supervisor, Carter, met with him to evaluate his first 90 days. "I thought you'd be further along. We hired you to deal with the problems of your predecessor. But, so far, it doesn't look like you've made any progress."

---

[1] This tracks. Gallup reports 51 percent of workers who leave their jobs claim the overriding factor was their boss.

Ryan Pendell, "6 Scary Numbers for Your Organization's C-Suite," Gallup. com, October 30, 2018, https://www.gallup.com/workplace/244100/ scary-numbers-organization-suite.aspx.

Larry asked Carter which metrics he was evaluating. Carter showed him twenty different metrics focused on revenue, retention, customer satisfaction, and employee engagement. He added, "You've only made progress in one of these areas."

When Larry asked him to identify the three most important metrics, Carter responded, "The three most important are all of them."

Confused and dejected, Larry left the meeting just as unclear on priorities. He knew he needed to think about the challenges and develop a plan, but where would he find the time? He determined he would devote his afternoon to strategic thinking when he got back to his office.

Instead, he was greeted by three of his direct reports sitting outside his door. Each of them had a challenge that would "only take a minute," but they absorbed the rest of his day. How in the world could he carve space for thinking strategically when he had so many fires to put out?

Larry's responsibilities had grown beyond what he could handle. He felt like he was treading water, going under, but he couldn't call out to anyone. Who could he even talk to? If he admitted how overwhelmed he felt, his boss and subordinates would lose confidence in him. (He already believed that their confidence was on shaky ground.) He couldn't tell his fellow senior managers, or they might report it to someone.

Besides that, everyone else appeared to have it all together. They were constantly *humble-bragging* about how great they were doing and how successful their teams were, even though employee engagement and retention scores said otherwise.

Larry was befuddled. He had always been a high performer. The guy people counted on. If he said, "I don't know what I'm doing," what would they think?

So, he kept going. More hours. More stress. More pretending.

His wife started to notice.

"Larry, what happened to you? This was supposed to be your 'dream role,' but you've been miserable since you got it. You're grumpy. You're always on your phone or computer. You don't laugh or smile much these days. Even when you're at the kids' baseball games, you're looking at your phone most of the time. Something has to change."

He knew she was right. But he didn't know what to do. His responsibilities kept piling up.

One night, at 1:27 a.m., Larry sat in his home office, staring at a blank notepad. He couldn't sleep, so he decided to build a task list for tomorrow.

- Develop next Quarter's plans for Carter
- Create a clear direction for the team
- Respond to emails

Three tasks in and already overwhelmed, he put down his pen. He could feel the pressure of the expanding whirlwind, one pressing need after the other spiraled inside his head. And the strain didn't end at work. His family needed his attention. His kids had felt the heat from his shortening fuse. His wife was asleep in bed without him.

In spite of all his previous accolades, Larry felt defeated and alone.

For the first time in his life, he was failing and had no idea what to do. He didn't know who to talk to or how to fix it. He put his head in his hands and sighed. With a heavy heart, Larry came to a conclusion. This belief rolled around in his head like a forlorn pinball circling to its finish. He finally said it out loud:

"I am a bad leader."

꼬⊙뀀

Does Larry's story sound familiar? Have you ever had similar thoughts? If so, you've picked up the right book.

You are not a bad leader. The fact that you looked for a book to get better at leading makes you a good one.

But you may be a leashed leader[IP].

ORIENTATION

1

How Leaders Become Leashed

A COUPLE OF years ago, our family attended a neighborhood party. A friend, Cory, challenged me (Garland) to a short race—just 30 yards. I enjoy a good competition, so I accepted.

The race began, and for the first 18 yards, my sprint went well. I even had a slight lead. Around the 20-yard mark, I felt a tug from behind but managed to press on for a couple more yards. Suddenly, I flew backward, tumbling in a messy, middle-aged somersault.

Here's what I haven't told you: I was attached to the cord of an inflatable bungee run. On this apparatus, two competitors wear a body harness attached to a thick bungee cord. The farther the participants run, the greater the bungee tension—until both fly heels over head backward on the tarp.

Cory and I immediately jumped up and yelled, "That was awesome!" I looked at him and exclaimed, "Let's do it again!"

Timmy, a 7-year-old in our neighborhood, protested, "Hey! It's my turn."

I turned to Timmy, "The grown-ups are having a little fun. Don't worry. You'll get your turn."

Round two was no different. Cory and I sprinted even harder, and the cord yanked us backward. This time, though, I landed even less gracefully. I flipped multiple times, my neck and back making unsettling cracks.

I stood up and stretched. The truth is, I was hurting. But I didn't want to wimp out.

"Want to do it again?" I asked Cory.

He agreed, though I could tell he was in a bit of pain, too.

Again, Timmy chimed in. "Hey, you can't go three times in a row."

Cory responded, "Hey, buddy, developing patience is one of the most important life skills."

By this attempt, I had learned my lesson. Instead of running as fast as I could, I ran just hard enough to stay ahead. When the inevitable tug occurred, I stopped running, hoping for a less violent yank.

Instead, the cord caught me again. I tripped and fell on my face, getting dragged several yards. As I stood up, I heard a gasp from the crowd of children. The right side of my face had been burned by the tarp.

Timmy shouted, "He looks like Two Face from *Batman*." All the children cackled.

Cory looked at me, "Up for one more race?"

"You know," I responded, "Timmy has been waiting so patiently. I think we need to let him race."

I had had enough. I didn't want to get injured again. After starting each sprint with enthusiasm, I had grown tired of picking myself up. Tired of the pain. After only three races, I decided to quit. The agony of falling down became greater than the joy of getting up and trying again.

It didn't matter how hard I ran. As long as I was leashed to a bungee cord, I could never win this game.

2

What Is the Leash?

LEADERSHIP CAN FEEL like you're strapped to a giant bungee cord. You run as hard as you can. Inevitably, something pulls you backward. You take five steps forward and get yanked back three. The next day, you make it ten steps and get pulled back eight. Another day, you only make it two steps and get dragged back ten steps.

> You become leashed when disparity exists between your responsibilities and abilities.[IP]

The challenges feel infinite, and every time you encounter one, you experience a disparity between your responsibilities and your abilities. This feeling is the sign that you are leashed.

You become leashed when disparity exists between your responsibilities and abilities.[IP]

Some Challenges That Leash You

- Losing a key team member
- Taking on too many projects
- Hiring and onboarding new people
- Managing change up, down, and laterally
- Fearing failure but needing to look confident
- Bickering team members who need to collaborate
- Underperforming direct reports who require training
- Changing roles when the organization restructures
- People-pleasing tendencies that undermine the mission
- Getting a new supervisor who has different expectations
- Cutting the budget and making hard personnel decisions
- Experiencing a crisis that suddenly changes your priorities
- Facing multiple, simultaneous challenges that you're unprepared for
- Managing the litany of endless meetings
- Not enough time to get things done

Two Ways That Disparity Manifests[IP]

Disparity manifests in two ways.

1. **Your abilities exceed current responsibilities.**
   Most people, at some point in their careers, find themselves in a position that doesn't challenge them enough. Their drive and innovation outpace the

cadence of the organization. It may even threaten the people they report to.

Ivy, a bright, personable new hire, felt this leash. Ivy's skills were undeniable. Not only was she competent in her industry knowledge, but Ivy also exhibited rare leadership talent. Despite her talent, Ivy hadn't been with the company long enough to "earn" a managerial position. She was leashed to a role that underutilized her abilities.

Like most people who are leashed to responsibilities less than their abilities, Ivy soon grew bored and disengaged. Her performance plummeted.

Although *Unleashed Leadership* can help you work through this first disparity, the framework addresses the second type of disparity the most.

2. **Your current responsibilities exceed your abilities.**

As you advance in your career, you, like Larry, may find your leadership abilities struggling to keep up with the responsibilities of your role. Your natural talent may have gotten you this far, but now increased demands hold you back.

When Matthew stepped into his new CEO role at a manufacturing plant, he quickly realized his responsibilities outpaced his abilities. Though he had previously led his division to major growth, this new challenge was different. He had been hired to triple revenue and profitability, but the plant was a mess. Employees cut corners, machines broke down from poor maintenance, and key leaders stalled projects due to miscommunication. Teams argued constantly, safety violations led to injuries, and customer reviews were scathing. The sales team had no system for tracking leads, and too many product lines diluted their focus.

Despite his past success, Matthew felt overwhelmed by the complexity of the problems.

We were able to help Ivy, Matt, and countless others because we've been there. We know what it's like to be leashed. *And* we developed a way out.

3

How We Became Unleashed

IN OUR EARLY twenties, we stepped into an opportunity that would change the course of our lives. We were hired by a family that not only had a successful national business but also funded a two-decade-old nonprofit foundation. Over time, one of the foundation's programs had lost focus. The family was expending massive resources, but no one quite knew what it was trying to accomplish. In fact, when we got there, no one could even agree on the name of the twenty-year-old program.

After months of wrestling, the family decided that they wanted the program to focus on leadership. This made sense. What set their business apart was its reputation, which rested equally on product excellence and a long legacy of cultivating leaders who drove results and cared deeply about people.

They tasked us with creating a four-year leadership development program for college students. We would also need to build a staff while ensuring we represented the family and their business well. Dorothy started off as director while Garland was still working on his master's degree. Later, when we started having kids, Garland took over as director, and Dorothy moved into a supporting role.

While we were thrilled with this new direction, we were also terrified. We knew nothing about leading others, much less about developing leaders. In truth, the family had hired us because we were young and cheap. We just happened to be in the right roles at the right time. If we stayed stagnant, we would be ill-equipped for and undeserving of our new roles. We had a lot of growing ahead of us and no idea where to begin.

We were leashed.

There was an undeniable disparity between the responsibilities we had been given and our abilities.

Thrust into leadership with no clue what we were doing—
our dog wasn't the only one who was leashed.

The Only Two Things Going for Us

Two qualities made up for our lack of knowledge: curiosity and passion. We began by reading leadership and management books—hundreds of them—attending conferences to learn from experts, and listening to hours of tapes and CDs (the best technology had to offer in the early 2000s).

The family opened their vast network to help us connect with leadership experts all over the country. We talked to business leaders who led multi-billion-dollar companies and nonprofit leaders with thousands of participants. Psychologists and therapists taught us about the mind and mindset of leaders. Philosophers and theologians helped us understand different leadership worldviews. We spoke to people who weren't well-known themselves but who had mentored hundreds of emerging leaders. Sports coaches shared how they developed a team atmosphere while working with competitive people. VPs of Learning taught us about how they identified and developed leadership potential. We interviewed C-Suite leaders of large companies to ask them what qualities they looked for in leaders.

With each new insight, we would gather our staff and spend hours debating and creating. It felt like we were responsible for putting together one cohesive puzzle while surrounded by the scattered pieces of ten puzzles.

It took two years of research and learning before we launched the first iteration of our leadership development program. After all that work and preparation, we were proud to hear seasoned leaders telling us that they wished they could participate.

But we weren't finished.

Developing Better Leaders

We spent the next decade continuing to refine the program and our own leadership. We would meet with our graduates to learn about gaps they were experiencing now that they were in the workforce. From these updates, we developed new tools that would help participants. We recognized that most leadership material is theoretical, so we partnered with educational leaders who taught us how to turn theories into practical applications.

All the while, we knew we couldn't *develop* better leaders until we *became* better leaders. We hired leadership coaches who helped us grow our strengths.

We recognized that many leadership deficiencies result from failing to deal with emotional issues. Our whole team worked with psychologists who specialized in helping leaders deal with their inner demons.

> Become a better leader before developing better leaders.[IP]

As our team grew, we realized that we weren't only developing individual leaders. We needed to develop teams of leaders. We worked with consultants to improve our teamwork and to help our students do the same with their teams.

As our passion for leadership development grew, so did our expertise. While Dorothy collected leadership coaching certifications, Garland earned his doctorate in leadership and spiritual formation. His studies focused on balancing the inner world of the leader with the results they need to achieve.

Then, after years of working to develop emerging leaders for the family's foundation, the unimaginable happened. The family split off into multiple foundations, and a new leader reorganized existing programs, including ours.

Going Out on Our Own

In 2017, we launched our business, AdVance Leadership. For fifteen years, we had heard leaders say that they wished they could participate in the program we had built. Now it was time to take our expertise out into the world.

Our focus needed to be on companies with 750 or more employees because larger organizations require a deep bench of leaders. Originally, companies would hire us to create and host multi-month leadership development opportunities. We hosted groups in places like Washington, DC, Atlanta, and Disney World using experiential learning to advance their leadership. (We still create these experiences for a handful of clients every year.)

Then, 2020 hit and killed face-to-face gatherings. Clients asked us to help their leaders deal with the unprecedented problems that emerged from the pandemic. They weren't sure what they needed, so they asked us to develop something for them.

After years of frustration, encountering too much "inspirational" and "motivational" leadership material, we decided to focus on a *practical* and *comprehensive* framework.

We chose *practical* because most leadership material is great at theory but terrible at helping you know how to implement the solutions. It's like watching a YouTube video of someone exclaiming how delicious a recipe is without explaining how to make it. We wanted to exclaim *and* explain–to create ridiculously practical tools that help leaders *do* what they need to do. In fact, we adopted the term, *ridiculously practical,* as one of our company's core values.

> The scale and intensity of the challenges varied, but the core leadership struggles remained the same.

We chose *comprehensive* for two reasons. First, most leadership materials zero in on a singular, tiny issue. If you peruse the management section of a bookstore, you'll find books that tell leaders how to craft a better vision, tell better stories, or be more creative. We've read hundreds of these books, and they are useful—*if you already know the skill your team needs you to develop or the root cause of your problems.*

But we kept hearing leaders say, "I don't know where to start." We wanted to develop a comprehensive solution to address the root causes plaguing leaders.

Second, we noticed a fascinating pattern. Regardless of industry, experience level, or company size, leaders struggled with the same fundamental challenges. A seasoned pastor running a church for 20 years faced the same issues as a first-time manager leading a small team. A Fortune 500 CEO wrestled with the same problems as a mid-level manager with 15 direct reports. The scale and intensity of the challenges varied, but the core leadership struggles remained the same.

The Seven Root Issues That Leash Leaders[IP]

We started by exploring a question: "What are the root issues in leadership that we have seen pop up over and over again?" We looked through two decades of our notes, conversations, consultations, coaching, and client interactions. From this research, we identified seven issues that cause 95 percent of leadership problems[IP].

Character	Clarity
Competence	Community
Capacity	Culture
Consistency	

In reality, we have *never* encountered a leadership problem that does not fit into these seven issues, making the actual percentage closer to 99.9 percent. We round down to leave space for potential new insights.

Next, we went a level deeper. For each of the seven issues, we identified best practices that quickly unleash leaders. We call these best practices "Breakaways[IP]" to convey an escape from the leash. These Breakaways helped us create something both practical and comprehensive.

Since creating the Unleashed Leadership framework, we have worked with thousands of leaders across a wide spectrum of industries: pest control, manufacturing, banking, medical supplies, law, food service, financial services, technology, retail, logistics, and fellow entrepreneurs, to name a few. We've helped individual leaders like you identify the issues holding them back and provided the tools and know-how to unleash their leadership.

Everything we've implemented with individual leaders, we've also accomplished with teams and entire companies. Most organizations have at least a couple of the seven issues running rampant. As the leaders within a company get unleashed, the whole company transforms.

Every time a leader gets more unleashed, everyone benefits.

- Their team enjoys work more and increases productivity.
- The company gets better results and builds a healthier culture.
- Customers grow more satisfied.
- Shareholders and investors become more profitable.

Before we dive into how to break free from these seven issues, we need to make a quick stop. In the next chapter, you'll understand what leadership is. You might assume you already know, but don't skip this chapter. Before you can get unleashed, you need a clear image of who you want to be.

4

Defining Leadership

IN 1964, THE Supreme Court attempted to define "obscenity" and "hard-core pornography" in order to determine what was legal. But the justices found this to be more difficult than they anticipated. Eventually, Justice Potter Stewart said, "I shall not further attempt to define the kinds of materials... but I know it when I see it."[2]

That type of ambiguity may work for the Supreme Court, but it doesn't work for the word "leader."

Imagine the CEO of your company calls you and a coworker into his office. The CEO says, "We need a *new sales leader*. You two work together to make it happen."

You get to work searching for a VP of Sales—someone who will oversee your team of salespeople.

However, your coworker starts researching on her own. She's trying to find a subject matter expert who trains others on how to sell more effectively.

You both work on this project separately for weeks until, one day, you share with each other the results of your searches. She looks confused when you show her your list of VP candidates. You are equally bewildered when she shows

---

[2]   Peter Lattman (September 27, 2007). "The Origins of Justice Stewart's 'I Know It When I See It'". *LawBlog at The Wall Street Journal Online*. Retrieved September 4, 2025.

you her list of trainers and coaches to hire as vendors. You both started with the same guidance: "We need a new sales leader."

The two of you return to the CEO and share your confusion. He, too, seems perplexed. He responds, "I don't want either of those. I mean that Joe has been the top salesperson for the last three months. We need a new sales leader who can compete with Joe."

All three of you had different definitions of the word *leader*. Those disparities in definitions drastically altered what each of you sought in a sales leader.

Socrates said, "The beginning of wisdom is the definition of terms." If you want to grow as a leader, it's essential to clarify what you mean by that word. Here are a few common opinions about what a leader is.

- A person who has a position or title (e.g., manager, vice-president, etc.)
- An influential individual who affects what other people think or do
- A loud, charismatic person who others pay attention to
- A confident, abrasive person who openly shares opinions
- A humble, unassuming person with high integrity
- The most popular or successful or productive person

That's just a sampling of what people believe a leader is. This wide assortment of definitions demonstrates why people hold different leaders in high esteem. It also shows why *you* have to know what *you* mean by leader. Defining what a leader is gives you an image to aspire toward. That definition affects who you want to become and how you desire to grow.

To help you get unleashed, we're going to share our definition of a leader.

While there's no perfect definition, here's how we define it at AdVance Leadership.

> **Definition of a Leader[IP]**
>
> A leader is someone who sees a clear, preferred, and desired future, who gathers others around that future, and who mobilizes others to create that future.

Let's break down these Three Facets of a Leader[IP].

Facet #1 Leaders See a Clear, Preferred, and Desired Future.[IP]

Leaders *must* see and focus on the future. This quality is often called *vision*. That vision must have three features.

1: The future must be clear.

Haddon Robinson, a professor of preaching, once said, "If a sermon is a mist in the pulpit, it will be a fog in the pew." The same is true for a leader: the future can't be fuzzy to you or those you lead. Your vision should be so clear that you can vividly describe it to others. If you or they aren't clear on the future, you can't lead them to it.

2: The future must be preferred.

Your vision of the future must be better than the present reality. If your vision is not perceived as better than their present, people will be disinterested. The future you envision must be preferred to the current situation, or people won't follow you there.

3: The future must be desired.

There's a difference between a *preferred* vision and a *desired* one. Preferences flow from the mind; desires come from the heart. A *preferred* vision makes people consider the change. A *desired* vision means they believe it's possible and want it so much that they will act on it. Both mind and heart must be engaged before hands activate.

In the 1920s and early 30s, Walt Disney built a company of artists who captured hearts and imaginations with their eight-minute, gag-filled cartoons. Yet, Walt had long recognized that the popularity of these short films had a limited shelf life.

For years, Walt envisioned an entirely new form of story-telling: full-length animated feature films. He believed they were inevitable and had spent years building a path for them. He started an art school so animators could enhance their skills and innovate with color, techniques, and technology.

The future was clear, preferred, and desired—but only by Walt. He needed the second facet: others who believe in that future.

Facet #2: Leaders Gather Others Around that Future

A vision with a one-member audience dies a quick death. If your vision is going to breathe life, you can't be the only one who sees it. You must assemble others alongside you who see it and want to make it happen.

In 1934, Walt made a unilateral decision to move forward with the creation of the first full-length cartoon, *Snow White and the Seven Dwarfs.* He began sharing this vision with others. Movie producers expressed little interest. Walt's brother, Roy, believed it would throw their company into bankruptcy. Influential film industry figures shunned it, referring to it as "Disney's Folly." Even his wife, Lilly, doubted the project.

Most people thought he was crazy. Walt knew that if his vision were to become a reality, others had to see it, too.

One night, Walt invited several of his animators to a sound stage. Illuminated by only one bulb, he acted out each part of *Snow White and the Seven Dwarfs* as it would appear on the screen. He used different voices and facial expressions for each character. At the end of his two-hour performance, the animators had tears in their eyes. (Tears are a strong indicator that people can see the vision.)

In the beginning, you don't need everyone to believe in your vision, but you do need to start with a few people who want to create that future together.

Walt Disney had the first two facets: a clear, preferred, and desired future and others gathered around that future. It was time for the third facet.

Facet #3: Leaders Mobilize Others to Create that Future

You've inspired a handful of people around that future. But that's not enough. Inspiration leaves people feeling warm and fuzzy, but it doesn't last long.

Instead, leaders *mobilize* people. They move them to take collaborative action to create the future together.

Walt assembled a team of animators right outside his office so that they could work together unencumbered.

He also found a few influential people in the film industry who supported the idea. This included W. G. Van Schmus, who managed the nation's largest movie theater, Radio City Music Hall. Before the film was completed, Van Schmus had already booked it for Radio City.

Walt also mobilized Joseph Rosenberg, the Bank of America executive who had previously loaned money to the studio. When Roy Disney asked for more money to complete the project, Rosenberg balked. He demanded that Walt show him the current work on *Snow White and the Seven Dwarfs.*

Even though Walt hated showing incomplete work, he brought Rosenberg a mashup of sequences. When the show finished, Rosenberg said to Walt, "That thing is going to make a hatful of money."

Walt mobilized the right people to help turn the vision into reality. In December 1937, *Snow White* premiered. Audiences flocked to theaters, pouring in $8 million while still recovering from the Great Depression, turning *Snow White* into the highest-grossing film at that time. The film also received an Academy Award, consisting of one large Oscar with seven smaller ones.[3]

The results of Walt's vision surpassed what even he had seen. Ushering in a seismic shift, *Snow White* changed the course of the entire film industry. It pushed technical and artistic boundaries and professionalized animation, proving that cartoons could be both art and business. *Snow White* set the standard for storytelling, paving the way for the flood of animated features that followed. If you've ever enjoyed a

---

[3]   Thomas, Bob. *Walt Disney: An American Original,* Kindle Edition. Disney Editions, 2017

full-length cartoon, you owe it to Walt Disney and his vision for *Snow White.*

 birth

To lead well, you need a clear vision of what it means to be a leader. It isn't about having a title or influencing others—it's about seeing a better future, gathering others around it, and mobilizing them to build it with you.

But it doesn't end there. If only it were that easy. No matter how well you epitomize this definition, seven issues threaten to leash even the most seasoned leaders.

5

The Seven Leadership Issues of a Leashed Leader

THE CHALLENGES OF leadership can seem infinite. No matter how well prepared you are, it can feel like you're never going to win. Leashed leaders can't win. Winning requires unleashing.

To get unleashed, you need to know and understand the seven issues that create at least 95 percent of the challenges you face. These are the leadership issues that hold you back from your greatest impact on your team, your company, and the world.

The first three issues—Character, Competence, and Capacity—require *self-development* and *inner work* from the leader. As you solve these issues, your work is unobservable, but the results can be felt by your team.

Team development issues happen when a leader fails to provide Clarity, Community, and Culture. The team experiences the negative effects of these issues, even if they can't name them. Solutions require everyone's participation.

The final issue, Consistency, encompasses both *self-development* and *team development*. Inconsistent leaders create chaos. This issue affects all the others, and the solutions work in tandem with the previous six.

The 7 Issues that Leash Leaders

1. **Character** issues arise when leaders act arrogantly, fail to take ownership of their responsibilities, or neglect accountability.
2. **Competence** issues emerge when leaders neglect their own self-knowledge and growth or attempt to use their old, proven skills to handle new roles or goals.
3. **Capacity** issues occur when leaders mismanage their time, energy, attention, or resources.
4. **Clarity** issues sabotage your team's ability to understand their priorities, plans, and roles.
5. **Community** issues stem from a perceived lack of safety, trust, and collaboration among team members.
6. **Culture** issues prevail when leaders tolerate attitudes and behaviors that undermine company values.
7. **Consistency** issues result when leaders routinely shift goals, change directions, or fluctuate expectations.

UNLEASHED LEADERSHIP[IP]

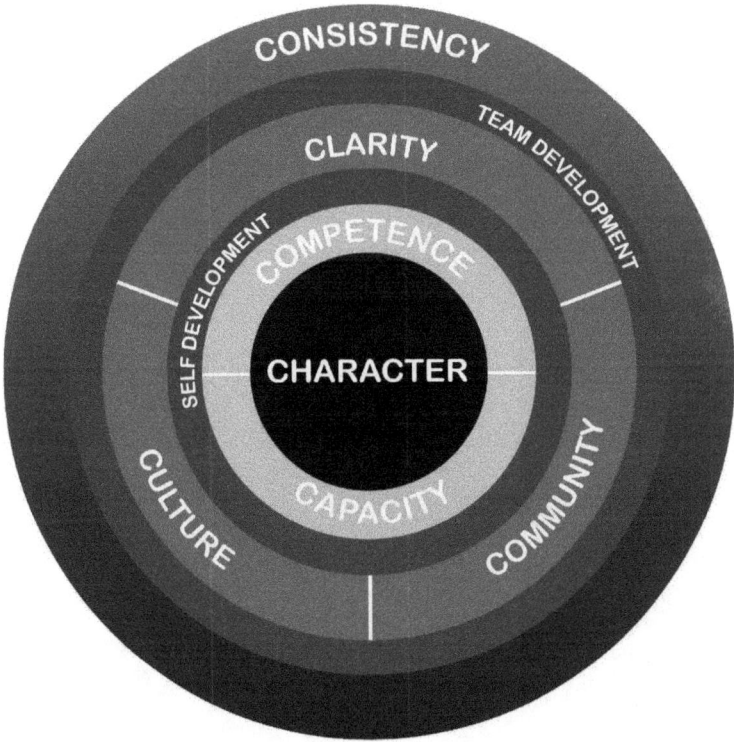

HOW TO GET
UNLEASHED

IN THE FOLLOWING sections, we will walk you through a three-stage process to unleash your leadership^{IP}.

In the first stage, you will Decide:

- If getting unleashed is worth it.
- If you will add conviction to your energy and effort.

In the second stage, Discern, you'll think deeply about what got you leashed. Don't worry, you won't need to talk to a therapist about this. Instead, you're going to use your noggin to:

- Name the presenting problems that are keeping you leashed.
- Identify the root leadership issues causing your presenting problems.
- Determine critical actions that will free you from those issues.

In the third stage, Deliver, you'll turn those critical actions into a plan. That plan will help you:

- Execute habits that will transform your leadership.
- Identify resources that will accelerate your growth.

THREE STAGES TO UNLEASH YOUR LEADERSHIP

01 DECIDE

☐ Evaluate if you are currently leashed (Chapter 2)

☐ Determine if it's worth it to get unleashed (Chapter 6)

☐ Choose your striving method (Chapter 7)

02 DISCERN

☐ Name the presenting problem(s) you're currently experiencing. (Chapter 8)

☐ Identify the underlying leadership issue(s) causing those problems. (Chapter 9)

1. Character
2. Competence
3. Capacity
4. Clarity
5. Community
6. Culture
7. Consistency

☐ Determine your critical actions. (Chapter 10)

03 DELIVER

☐ Activate your critical actions (Chapter 11)

☐ Accelerate your unleashing (Chapter 12)

Stage 1: Decide

01

DECIDE

☐ Evaluate if you are currently leashed
(Chapter 2)

☐ Determine if it's worth it to get
unleashed
(Chapter 6)

☐ Choose your striving method
(Chapter 7)

LONG AGO, IN a galaxy that might seem far away, you made important decisions. You may have recognized them as life-changing decisions, but they were also *world-changing decisions*. You're about to make one more.

Before we introduce your next decision, let's start with a look back on world-changing decisions you may have made in your life so far. You decided to:

- Get married. Or stay single. Or get divorced.
- Be an active parent. Or a disengaged parent. Or not to have children at all.
- Attend college. Or forgo college. Or start down a career path.

Your choices changed your future, your family's future, and generations to follow, the future of your coworkers, your company, and your customers. Cascading to countless people, your decisions ripple through the lives of people you've never met, some you'll never even share the planet with. Your decisions changed the world.

> Leaders change the world.[IP]

At some point, you decided to *be a leader*. You may not have thought of yourself as one, but you accepted a *position* that relies on followers. You took on the responsibility of managing others' lives. By choosing to be a leader, your world-changing influence expanded.

Whether you see it or not, when you decided to lead, you changed the world.

Your decisions change the world because they're not just about you. Whenever you implement change in your life (good or bad), your growth or decline reaches out and nudges (sometimes shoves) everyone around you. When the people around you shift, those adjustments impact everyone they affect. The chain reaction of your decisions is endless. The decision you're about to make will change the world.

If you read Garland's first book, *Gettin' (un)Busy*, you may remember his 5-step process that also started with "Decide."[4] Anytime you move toward change, your first step will always be to decide. Before you can *do* anything, you must resolve that you *want* to do it.

We humans run on the fuel of desire. It's up to us to choose what desires we fill our tanks with. We can't move with empty tanks.

Unleashing your leadership is change. Before you can take action and break away, you must decide you want to be an unleashed leader[IP].

This first stage, Decide, will help you determine if it's worth wanting.

---

[4]   Garland Vance, *Gettin' (Un)Busy: 5 Steps to Kill Busyness and Live with Purpose, Productivity, and Peace* (Powell, OH: Author Academy Elite, 2019).

6

Is Getting Unleashed Worth It?

AFTER YOU'RE GONE, your children may be able to write a book about you, your grandchildren may be able to tell a story about you, and your great-grandchildren may remember your name.

Memories of you may not last long, but your legacy will. Legacy is bigger than who you are. Legacy is the lasting effects of what you do.

If you choose to stay leashed, both your legacy and the legacy of your company are at stake.

Your Legacy

Have you ever worked with a leader who made your life worse? We both have. Have you worked for:

- A sexist bully?
- An insecure, petty leader who took credit for your ideas?
- A power-hungry tyrant who was only in it for their own advancement?
- Workaholics who cared nothing about you personally or professionally?

- Managers who viewed people as expendable cogs in a machine?
- An outright abuser who attempted to strip you of any sense of self-worth?
- Someone who simply never saw you? Who never acknowledged your contributions or drew out your potential?

If you've been in the working world for more than a second, we can guess that your answer to at least one of these questions is a resounding "yes!"

Think of that person (or people) for a second. Not too long, or you risk becoming angry or depressed. Think about how they treated you and how they made you feel about yourself.

- Did you go home and talk about that person at the dinner table?
- Did they influence the way you felt about yourself?
- Did they change the way you treated others?
- What did your family and friends notice about how this person affected you?

In the story of your life, that "leader" was a villain.

Now, think about the opposite. Think about a leader who cared about you, who challenged you to be better, *and* supported you in achieving it. These leaders are rare, but they leave a lasting impression.

For me (Garland), Phil was one of those leaders. He and I would meet monthly to talk about progress around my priorities. Phil always asked about my personal life and goals. For over a year, I told him that one of my dreams was to earn a doctorate. I once said to him, "If I haven't earned a doctorate by the time I die, I'm going to be deeply disappointed in myself."

He regularly encouraged me to research programs and make a plan. I confided in him that my biggest obstacles were finances and time. We were living off a low-paying, nonprofit salary and had three young children. We could barely afford the basics, much less tuition. I also didn't want to take my limited vacation time away from my family to attend classes.

After several months of these conversations, Phil called me to share some news. He had helped launch a continuing education initiative. The foundation

> Every leader is a hero or villain.[P]

would fund half of my tuition and books and provide comp time to attend classes. Phil enabled me to accomplish a big dream and helped me overcome obstacles that got in the way.

Have you had that kind of boss?

- Did you go home and talk about that person at the dinner table?
- Did they influence the way you felt about yourself?
- Did they change the way you treated others?
- What did your family and friends notice about how this person affected you?

In the story of your life, that leader was a hero.

Every leader ever cast in your life script has played the role of a hero or a villain.

The same is true for all those who follow you.

You will either be a hero or a villain to every person you lead. You can't control what they think of you, but you can control how you view, treat, and support them. You can also control whether or not you get unleashed.

Your people need you to be a hero.

A leashed leader leaves a villainous legacy.
An unleashed leader leaves a heroic legacy.

Your Company's Legacy

We've got bad news to share, and it's the kind that stings. We're not ones to dwell on negativity, but this is something every leader needs to hear.

Are you ready? Brace yourself.

Every problem in your company starts as a leadership problem. Every issue on your team, in your division, and throughout your company can be traced back to:

- Opportunities leaders take advantage of or pass over
- How leaders talk about customers
- Leaders' treatment of employees
- Bad behavior leaders tolerate
- Leaders' allocation of money
- Strategies leaders deploy
- Decisions leaders make
- Actions leaders take
- People leaders hire

> Every problem starts with leadership.[IP]

We'll say it again: *Every problem in your company starts as a leadership problem.* If you don't believe us, let us remind you of a familiar story that illustrates how important leadership is.

Blockbuster to Lackluster

When we were growing up, Blockbuster Video was one of the happiest places on earth. Even though we weren't near each other—Dorothy down in Florida, Garland up in North Carolina—we share memories of perusing Blockbuster aisles every weekend with our friends. We'd browse hundreds of movies and pick out an armful to take home for the weekend. We '90s kids spent Friday nights in front of gargantuan cubed TVs, eating pizza and binge-watching videos before "binge-watching" was even a term. Blockbuster was a cultural staple of our generation.

Today, Blockbuster is known for something else—its near-total collapse. (At the time of this writing, it has one remaining store in Bend, Oregon.) At its peak in the early 2000s, Blockbuster had nearly 9,000 stores and employed around 84,000 people globally. In 2004, it was a $5.9 billion giant. Six years later, it filed for bankruptcy.[5]

How does such a prominent company fall so fast? The short answer: because every problem in your business starts as a leadership problem.

During the massive slide from 2000 to 2010, Blockbuster's leaders made several key mistakes.

Ignoring Competitors: Netflix started as a DVD-by-mail service, offering a more convenient option than brick-and-mortar. Blockbuster's leaders dismissed Netflix, assuming the old model would prevail.

---

[5] "The Sad End Of Blockbuster Video: The Onetime $5 Billion Company Is Being Liquidated As Competition From Online Giants Netflix And Hulu Prove All Too Much For The Iconic Brand," *International Business Times*, accessed June 18, 2025, https://www.ibtimes.com/sad-end-blockbuster-video-onetime-5-billion-company-being-liquidated-competition-online-giants

Infuriating Customers: Blockbuster relied on late fees for nearly $800 million per year of its annual revenue. Customers hated these fees, but they accounted for 16% of their top line. When Netflix emerged, they took advantage of customers' primary dissatisfaction with Blockbuster and didn't charge despised late fees.

Missing the Digital Shifts: Even as streaming became the future, Blockbuster clung to its retail stores. While competitors embraced the digital age, Blockbuster lagged.

Leveraging Too Much Debt: Blockbuster took on massive debt to expand its stores. When the market shifted, they couldn't keep up with their financial obligations.

Missing Opportunities: Perhaps the biggest "what if" in business history—Blockbuster had the chance to buy Netflix for $50 million in the early 2000s. They passed.

What do all these mistakes have in common? They started with the decisions and actions of leaders.

Leaders at Blockbuster placed bets they believed they would win, which ultimately led to the company's demise. These choices led to 84,000 people needing new jobs.

Every Problem in Your Business Includes Your Leadership

It's easy to shake our heads at these Blockbuster leaders and say, "How could they not see what was coming?" But the truth is, every leader faces critical decisions where people's livelihoods hang in the balance. Only time will tell if these decisions are good bets. Unfortunately, sometimes, leaders get them wrong.

Our intent is not to shame Blockbuster's former leaders. Instead, this story reminds us of the power of leadership and the harsh reality that every problem in your business is influenced by *your* leadership.

Read slowly over that last line.

If you picked up this book, it means that you are a leader. And that means *every problem includes you.*

We know it hurts to hear that your leadership is involved in every problem your business faces. It hurts us to say it. We've experienced that sting firsthand.

The first time we hired a consultant, it was in the early years of our nonprofit work. We were thrilled to gain an outside perspective, someone who could validate that we were under-resourced and undersupported, that there wasn't much we could do while trapped within the foundation's systemic issues. Instead, he shut down our complaints.

"I'm not here for the leaders above you," he said. "I'm here for you and your leadership. As long as you're leaders in this organization, you're contributors to the problems."

Ouch. That stung.

He continued, "I know it's comforting to focus on your constraints. But there's always something you can do. Every leader has the power to instigate solutions."

When we first told you that business problems start with leadership, you may have been tempted to think, "These issues aren't my fault; they're someone else's."

Not only have we seen this finger-pointing in ourselves, but we often see this in the early stages of working with a company. The front-line employee blames the team leader... who blames the shift leader... who blames the general manager... who blames the region manager... who blames the Vice President... who blames the Senior Vice President... who blames the CEO... who blames the front-line employee.

It's easy to waste time on blame, whether it be blaming others or yourself. A blaming mindset doesn't help you solve anything. An ownership mindset opens the gate for moving forward. Taking ownership is not the same as self-blame. Blame says, "I'm responsible for *causing* the problem." Ownership says, "I'm responsible for *solving* the problem." (More about this in book 2, *Unleashed Character.*)

> You have the power to change your leadership.

Anytime our business has a challenge, we look in the mirror and wave "hello" to the people behind the problems. (We may even repeat the words of the great philosopher, Taylor Swift, "It's me. Hi. I'm the problem. It's me."[6])

You can't fix someone else's leadership, but you can fix your own. Recognizing this truth empowers you to solve the problems.

You have the power to change your leadership. You have the power to get unleashed. Your business needs you to get unleashed because every problem in your business bears the imprint of your leadership.

So what do you think? Is your legacy and the legacy of your company worth it?

---

[6] "Anti-Hero" by Taylor Swift, *Midnights*, produced by Taylor Swift and Jack Antonoff. Republics Records, released October 21, 2022.

Five Common Reasons People Decide It's Not Worth It

Reason #1: Time

You may say: "I'm so busy. I don't have time for anything other than responding to the urgency of the day."

Ask Yourself: "How much time am I already losing by choosing to stay leashed?"

Reason #2: Knowledge

You may say: "I'd like to be unleashed. But I don't know how. I don't know how to escape the leash."

Ask Yourself: "Do I have to know all the details of how to do something before I decide to do it? Or will I trust this process?"

Reason #3: Support

You may say: "My organization does not provide support, financial or otherwise, for growth and development. The leaders above me don't care about my growth."

Ask Yourself: "Am I willing to stay leashed because others around me are leashed? Or do I value myself and those I lead enough to do what's best for all of us?"

Reason #4: Pain

You may say: "I've been leashed for a while. I've gotten used to it. How hard is this change going to be?"

Ask Yourself: "Has your team gotten used to your leash? Is the pain of you getting unleashed worth your team benefiting from an unleashed leader?"

Reason #5: Risk

You may say: "I'm the only one around me trying to get unleashed. Will I outgrow my company? Will I be a threat to those who lead me? Will I seem insubordinate?"

Ask Yourself: "Which is worse? To outgrow my company? Or to limit my potential to fit my company?"

7

Decide How to Drive Your Strive

ON ONE OF our daily walks, we passed an energetic dog leashed to his elderly owner. As we approached, it was clear from the way he pulled the gentleman along that the dog did not appreciate his constraint. As we passed, he noticed us (new, exciting people!) and bounced with glee, trying to keep up with our pace.

> Striving is made up of energy and effort. Conviction is the direction of that energy and effort.

His leash tugged him back.

A few minutes later, we looked down to discover the same dog next to us, unleashed and giddy. That smart little sucker had figured out how to break his confinement and keep step with walkers more his speed. He had made the decision to get unleashed. But he made it with *conviction*.

The dog couldn't help but strive. He was wired that way. Striving is made up of energy and effort. But he could choose how to direct his energy and effort. Conviction is the direction of that energy and effort. The dog could have chosen several different options.

1. Reign himself back to his owner's pace.
2. Wrestle with the leash haphazardly.
3. Figure out how to escape his confinement.

We've been working with leaders like you for a quarter century and have met thousands of them. Almost every one of them is like our doggie friend—having an overflow of energy.

We're guessing you're like these other leaders we know. You can't tone down your energy, so you're constantly trying to figure out where to direct it. You are a natural striver. You've decided to get unleashed, so you will strive for it. But just because you're striving doesn't mean you'll get anywhere. If you don't direct your energy appropriately, your energy will get you nowhere.

To get unleashed, you have a choice between Three Types of Striving[IP].

Choice 1:
Decision + No Conviction = Stalled Striving

My (Dorothy's) first car was a cute little white Volkswagen Cabriolet convertible that I loved. By the time Garland and I got married, the car was over ten years old, and the stick shift's gear lever had a habit of catching. Garland had never driven a manual transmission before, but I was determined to teach him so we could keep my beloved car. He, however, was not determined to learn. He lacked conviction.

After several discouraging lessons, Garland attempted to zip across four lanes of oncoming traffic when the scourge of any stick-shift vehicle occurred: the dreaded STALL. The steering wheel stiffened. The car bucked, jerked, and stopped.

The last thing you want when crossing four lanes of oncoming traffic is for your engine to shut off.

70

We both screamed, an eighteen-wheeler blaring its horn, barreling right for us. Somehow, the semi managed to swerve and avoid us. Garland restarted the car and scooted on out of the way. You've probably guessed the end of this story. We sold my VW.

A stick shift's engine shuts off when the clutch is released too quickly. Stalling happens when the load on the engine is greater than it is capable of overcoming. Cars stall because of *misdirected energy*. So do leaders. Your energy has to be directed somewhere. When the gas is pouring in but the wheels aren't turning, you stall out.

Stalled Striving is a type of striving. It happens when you *decide to get unleashed but with zero conviction*. You aspire to become unleashed. You intend to use your energy and effort toward that end.

Then, Monday morning comes. You go back to the office and encounter a couple of obstacles. You concede to constraints, avoid risks, or don't voice your opinion. All of your energy and effort are absorbed into the strain of holding back, rather than the movement of unleashing your leadership. You give up. You stall out.

With Stalled Striving, you waste energy and time. Eventually, you become exhausted and disillusioned. Striving without conviction keeps you leashed.

Choice 2:
Decision + Blind Zeal = Scattershot Striving

The term "scattershot" derives from a shotgun, which shoots pellets over a wide range. Instead of zeroing in on a target, bullets rain everywhere, hoping one will hit the mark.

Scattershot Striving follows a decision to become unleashed, but it's coupled with blind zeal. Blind zeal is *intense passion without knowledge or understanding of how to direct that passion.* With Scattershot Striving, you commit to becoming unleashed while being unclear about how you will do it.

Scattershot Striving occurs in two scenarios:

1. **You aim for multiple targets at the same time.** In this scenario, you're trying to accomplish too much, too quickly. When you have a legion of issues that require change, the likelihood of remedying any one of them drops dramatically.[7]
2. **You don't commit to a specific plan.** When helping leaders wriggle their way out of a leash, one of the first questions we ask is, "What have you tried?" For those who practice Scattershot Striving, there is no shortage of answers. The leader inevitably lists off one failed attempt after another.

Rarely, though, have they crafted a plan and stuck with it. Rather, like throwing spaghetti against a wall to see what sticks, they've attempted a dozen short-term solutions and seen them fail.

Choice 3:
Decision + Conviction = Strategic Striving

In 1990, the first cancer-treating proton center opened. Since then, proton beam therapy has become one of the

---

[7] According to *The 4 Disciplines of Execution,* when you have between four and ten goals, you only have a 20% chance of accomplishing one of them. But if you have three or fewer areas to focus on, you have a 95% chance of accomplishing all of them.Chris McChesney et al., *The 4 Disciplines of Execution: Achieving Your Wildly Important Goals* (New York, NY: Simon & Schuster Paperbacks, an imprint of Simon & Schuster, Inc, 2022).

most groundbreaking achievements in radiation technology. Instead of showering radiation over an affected area, damaging healthy tissue, cancer cells are pinpointed and targeted. My dad (Dorothy's) is still with us today, cancer-free and thriving, because of this treatment.

Imagine that concentrated stream of high-energy protons zeroed in on a tumor. This is the picture of Strategic Striving— energy and effort proactively predetermined and focused. While this might seem like common sense, it is not common practice.

Strategic Striving demands that you not only get clear on your intended outcome but also develop and execute an intentional plan.

Will you add conviction to your decision to get unleashed? If the answer is yes, keep reading. The rest of this book will map out a guide for your Strategic Striving.

Stage 2: Discern

02

DISCERN

☐ Name the presenting
problem(s) you're currently
experiencing.
(Chapter 8)

☐ Identify the underlying
leadership issue(s) causing
those problems.
(Chapter 9)

1. Character
2. Competence
3. Capacity
4. Clarity
5. Community
6. Culture
7. Consistency

☐ Determine your critical actions.
(Chapter 10)

ON NOVEMBER 23, 2016, high winds picked up sparks from teenagers' matches on one of our favorite hiking trails, the Chimney Tops, in our beloved Smoky Mountains. Over the next several days, the fire grew to uncontrollable strength, destroying property and taking 14 lives.

Some experts attribute the fire's devastation to thick layers of underbrush built up from years of extinguishing smaller fires. In an effort to control the immediate problem in front of them, foresters had been inadvertently growing a massive fuel source to feed a future wildfire. It took 21 days to fully extinguish.[8]

Forest floors are littered with layers of combustible materials—decaying vegetation, rotting trees and branches, dry leaves. On a walk through the woods, you pay attention to the life abounding around you. You may not notice the blanket of death beneath your feet. If those layers are allowed to build for too long and conditions (like a dry season and heavy winds) become just right, all of that decay can ignite with a single spark.

Leaders are often referred to as fire fighters. Every day, you stand with your fire hose at the ready, extinguishing each challenge as it flares up. You identify the quickest fix and then move on to the next issue. Unfortunately, this approach, often called "putting out fires," is not sustainable and doesn't result in permanent solutions. At best, it shrinks fires from a rage to a smolder. At worst, fires feed off festering underbrush.

In leadership, putting out fires rarely works because it fails to address the layers of buildup beneath. Relentless firefighting leads to discouragement. Discouragement leashes.

[8] Rosalia Otaduy-Ramirez, "The Chimney Tops 2 Fire," ArcGIS Story Maps, April 22, 2021, https://storymaps.arcgis.com/stories/335e51f69e7f4c62b330a4febb8469ca.

You may have tried to untangle yourself from discouragement by browsing the internet or Amazon for answers. But how do you know where to start? *Your true issues are hidden in the underbrush.*

Foresters have learned to combat the danger of buildup with controlled burns. They identify the source of the potential hazard hidden beneath a camouflage of debris and destroy the fuel load before it takes on a life of its own.

In battling their own fires, many leaders feel overwhelmed by the time and effort it would take to identify the source. It may have relieved you to have read earlier that, in our years of research, we have uncovered only seven issues that cause leadership challenges. You don't have to dig endlessly with no idea what you're searching for. Put away the hose. Get out your shovel. Brush that deceptive top layer aside, and discern which of these pesky seven keeps flaring up.

8

Name the Presenting Problems

TAMARA, A FOOD service professional, was hired by a local business owner, Mr. Patel, to lead a team that would provide premade meals to harried families. Each weeknight, customers stopped by to pick up their preordered dish of the day to heat up at home.

In the past few months, sales had dropped. This decrease in sales was Tamara's first alert to her presenting problem – her *surface-level* pain point. Her first recognition that something's on fire.

Tamara immediately grabbed her extinguisher and started spraying. *Sales have decreased! Must be a marketing issue!* She initiated a social media blitz, inundating her community with ads. For a brief period, sales picked up, but then they dropped again. She asked a team member to initiate a customer satisfaction survey with anyone who had used their services.

When the survey results came in, Tamara was pleased with the quality ratings. Most people raved about the taste of the food. They believed prices were fair for what they received. In fact, they were disappointed that they had to cancel.

From the survey, Tamara discovered that meals had not been ready by the time promised. Customers had been showing up between errands, a car loaded with perishables, a toddler waiting at daycare, expecting to run in and out. Instead, they were greeted with an apology and—

"Your meal's not quite ready yet. You're welcome to wait. Or you can come back later. It shouldn't be any longer than another hour."

Tamara finally had her answer. Customers were quitting because their meals weren't available when promised. They had lost trust in the business.

Tamara thought, *I know what this is. I do not have enough people to get meals out on time. I've got to hire more people!*

Tamara stepped back from some of her responsibilities to interview for two new positions. By the time she found strong candidates and onboarded them, two more months had passed. But at least now the issue would be solved. With two extra bodies in the kitchen, meals would now be ready when promised.

Another month passed. Sales continued to decline. This time, Tamara personally called customers who had discontinued to ask why they were canceling.

She heard things like, "The food is delicious. I really wish it worked. This kind of service could be so helpful to my family. But, honestly, it's just a crap shoot if the meals are going to be ready when it's time to pick them up."

Tamara was shocked. She had hired two more meal-preppers! How were they still missing the deadlines? And how was she unaware that meals were habitually late?

Sinking into discouragement, Tamara began to question her ability to lead. Everything she had tried had failed. *I can't even figure out what the real issue is,* she thought. *Does that mean I'm the problem?* As her concerns escalated, Tamara grew fearful that Mr. Patel might realize her inadequacies and let her go. She had to do something. But where to begin?

࿎

Do Tamara's challenges resonate with you? She saw a fire burning—a decrease in sales—and reacted. She grabbed the nearest extinguisher and started dousing—anything to smother the flames as quickly as possible. By operating with urgency, Tamara wasted months ignoring the source of what was keeping the sparks smoldering. She felt the tug of the leadership leash, the pull of her responsibilities exceeding her current abilities.

Tamara voiced her frustrations to a friend, sharing her feelings of helplessness. Her friend, a subscriber to our Friday 411 newsletter, forwarded her an Unleashed Leadership article. Tamara delved into the process, finally hopeful that she wouldn't have to engage in an endless search for solutions. There were only seven possibilities.

Step 1: Name the Presenting Problem(s)

Your first step is to pinpoint your current pain point(s) and accept them as issues that require addressing. These symptoms could include:

- Increased customer cancellations
- High employee disengagement
- Failing to meet deadlines
- Low employee retention
- Diminished profitability
- Low productivity
- Lagging sales

Make a list of the presenting problems that you're currently experiencing. You might not be able to address all these symptoms at the same time. But you can't deal with problems unless you know what they are. You can't truly know what they are if you can't name them.

This step should be easy. These problems have been taunting you for weeks, months, maybe years. Every time you thought you annihilated them, they crept back up. You may have read books about them, been coached on how to conquer them, and attended conferences. They haunt you. You resent them. You *hate* these problems. At this point, you have put enough thought into your problems to know their names.

Tamara could quickly name her presenting problems: customer retention, not getting meals out on time, decreased sales, reduced revenue, and reduced profitability. These pain points had been keeping her up at night for months.

As soon as you name your presenting problems, you can move on to the second step.

Want to check out the Friday 411 newsletter? Scan here.

9

Identify the Underlying Leadership Issue(s)

THE SECOND STEP can be tricky and requires a bit more effort than the first. It reminds me (Dorothy) of the first time I did yard work in our current home. After a day of hard labor clearing brush, my arms started itching. My skin sprouted ugly red welts, and the rash spread.

My presenting problem was an itchy rash. If I were to ever work in our backyard again, I had to get rid of the source of my problem. If I didn't, I would risk this horrific malady every time I did yardwork. I was allergic to something but knew nothing about plants. I couldn't avoid the cause of my problem without the ability to recognize it.

After a quick online search, I determined that, in my region, poison ivy was the most likely offender. I studied descriptions of identifiers and pictures of the plant. Sure enough, I located vines of telltale "leaves of three" climbing up a trellis. Now, I could eliminate the cause of my rash so it would not reoccur.

Moving through the second step of the Discern stage will dig up one or more root leadership issues that cause your presenting problems. In fact, most presenting problems could be an indicator of *any* of the Unleashed Leadership issues.

Let's examine how Tamara's presenting problems (customer retention, not getting meals out on time, decreased sales, reduced revenue, and reduced profitability) could stem from any of the Unleashed Leadership issues. In the middle column, you'll find a list of several possible indicators of each issue. In the right column is a description of what these issues would look like if they were behind Tamara's presenting problems.

Leadership Issue Chart[IP]

Leadership Issue	Indicators of Issues	Tamara
Character	The leader fails to: • Treat others well • Take ownership of responsibilities • Deal with difficult situations or conversations	Blames external factors (like staff and "bad customers") instead of looking inward to assess how she can improve
Competence	The leader neglects: • Growing in their own self-knowledge • Understanding how to support the team and company in achieving goals • Acquiring skills necessary for their role	Continues applying the same solutions to different problems even though they stopped working
Capacity	The leader mismanages: • The energy necessary to perform with excellence • The time needed to focus on priorities • The resources required to get work done through others	Takes on all the work without relying on and empowering her team
Clarity	The team does not know: • What they're trying to accomplish • How to achieve their goals • Each person's role in their goals	Has not solidified or communicated goals, priorities, processes, or roles
Community	The team lacks: • A sense of psychological and physical safety • Trust with the leader and each other • The willingness and ability to collaborate	Ignores the emotional and relational needs of her team
Culture	The team demonstrates: • Behaviors that do not align with company values • Tolerance for poor attitudes • Habits and actions that undermine company ethos	Overlooks staff behaviors that contradict ideals and beliefs the company stands for
Consistency	The leader and the team erratically shift: • Goals when they don't reach them quickly • Priorities when urgency takes over • Expectations when they become inconvenient	Changes goals, priorities, or expectations on a whim

When an issue arises, few leaders pause and do the necessary work to discover what is feeding the flame. It is okay to let a problem smolder a bit while you identify what would smother it for good. If you don't tackle the undergrowth of your presenting problems, where the blaze is being fueled, you will lose revenue and profit. You will frustrate customers and staff members. You won't sleep well at night. Your leadership will stay leashed.

You may have noticed that "communication" is not one of the traits. This often surprises people for two reasons. First, communication is frequently cited as the primary culprit behind teams' struggles. Second, communication starts with a C.

However, in our research, we have found that poor communication is never the root cause of the leadership problem. Rather, communication is a presenting problem that can be categorized under any of the seven issues. Check out this article to find out two reasons communication is never the real issue on your team.

When Tamara reacted without identifying the source, her marketing initiatives were like dribbling a garden hose on spreading flames. They didn't soak through to where the problem began. Tamara now knew that she had a lot more investigating to do before she could solve her problem. She assembled her team to help her dig.

Tamara came into the meeting with a presupposition that she was dealing with a Competence issue. Her first instinct had been that her marketing was failing. Now she was convinced that her own ability to lead was inadequate. She must not have provided the proper training to her employees.

"You all have got to help me understand what's happening," Tamara told them. "How are we still not meeting deadlines? Was there something I missed in the training?"

Her four employees exchanged glances.

Finally, Sue spoke up. "Can we be honest?"

"Yes! Please!" Tamara answered.

The others gave Sue an encouraging look. She swallowed. "Tamara, you have a gift for creating recipes. I know you spent a lot of time perfecting them. Your meals are delicious. It's no wonder we've had such an easy time gaining customers. People tell everyone they know how good your food is."

"And you train us well," Emily insisted. "Every day, you walk us through exactly what we need to make and how to make it."

The others nodded in agreement.

"I sense a 'but' here," Tamara prompted.

"But," Sue continued. "You esteem excellence so highly that we sacrifice efficiency."

Tamara cinched her eyebrows in confusion.

"Last Thursday!" Emily jumped in helpfully.

The others chimed in, "Yes, Thursday!"

Emily went on, "Last Thursday, we were almost through with meal prep. We were going to make the deadline. We were boxing everything up, ready to get it to the door for pickup. Then you came around and noticed the chives on the shepherd's pie were *slightly* wilted. And you didn't think the ratio was right. So you had us strip all the chives. Remember? And then chop fresh chives. Then, you started questioning the other ingredients because the chives hadn't met your standards."

"Yes," Sue interjected. "You didn't even notice the clock. You made it clear that getting the recipes perfect was more important than anything else."

"Deadlines are important, too," Tamara countered. "How did I lead you to believe they weren't?"

Sue responded, "Because you don't say anything about deadlines. All you care about in the moment is making sure the dish looks beautiful."

Tamara couldn't argue with them. She knew herself well enough to know she wasn't good at noticing the time.

"And as long as we're talking," Emily looked at the two new hires, Peter and Christina, apologetically. "You guys are great. Nothing against either of you. But I think adding two more people has actually slowed us down. Too many cooks in the kitchen, you know? We're all over each other, all doing the same thing."

"What?" Tamara exclaimed. "Do we need a bigger workspace?"

I thought Capacity was an issue, Tamara thought. *I just got the resource wrong. It's space, not people.*

Emily held up her hand. "No! No, no, no. It's not that at all. We need..." Emily struggled to find the right words.

"We need..." Sue tried.

"We need to know what you want most—what's most important," Christina offered.

"Yes!" Sue and Emily agreed.

Sue explained, "You haven't been clear on what you want from us. What is most important to the business? What do you want us to prioritize? It would be great if we could have excellence and efficiency all the time. But that's not realistic right now. When a choice has to be made, we've been choosing excellence. But we're losing customers over that choice."

Clarity! Tamara realized. *I haven't taken the time to communicate priorities to my team. Do I even know what our company values are? What would Mr. Patel rather I do? Wait for perfection but deliver late? Or meet deadlines with subpar meals?*

"I know I'm new," Peter chimed in. "But what if we didn't have to choose between excellence and efficiency?"

The others turned to him, questioning.

"In my time here, I've noticed you guys are reinventing the wheel every day. A lot of what we do is the same—even making the same recipes—but we always start from scratch. If we documented our repeatable processes, we could get things done a lot faster."

"That would be wonderful," Emily agreed.

"Tamara, maybe you could build... like a step-by-step book with photos?" Christina suggested. "That way, we could see exactly what each dish should look like. We'd be more likely to meet your excellence standard without losing efficiency."

They're talking about Consistency, Tamara realized. *I've got some work to do. But I know where to start.*

Tamara finally saw past the presenting problems and recognized her two underlying leadership issues: Clarity and Consistency.

∽⊙⑤∾

What about you? Go through each of the indicators below to see which ones are true of your current leadership and presenting problems.

Leadership Issue	Indicators of Issues	You
Character	The leader fails to: • Treat others well • Take ownership of responsibilities • Deal with difficult situations or conversations	
Competence	The leader neglects: • Growing in their own self-knowledge • Understanding how to support the team and company in achieving goals • Acquiring skills necessary for their role	
Capacity	The leader mismanages: • The energy necessary to perform with excellence • The time needed to focus on priorities • The resources required to get work done through others	
Clarity	The team does not know: • What they're trying to accomplish • How to achieve their goals • Each person's role in their goals	
Community	The team lacks: • A sense of psychological and physical safety • Trust with the leader and each other • The willingness and ability to collaborate	
Culture	The team demonstrates: • Behaviors that do not align with company values • Tolerance for poor attitudes • Habits and actions that undermine company ethos	
Consistency	The leader and the team erratically shift: • Goals when they don't reach them quickly • Priorities when urgency takes over • Expectations when they become inconvenient	

What did you find? Where has your digging led you? Now that you've followed the flames, dug through the underbrush, and revealed the smoldering embers beneath, your issues are no longer hidden.

You're staring right at them. This is where you may be tempted to turn tail and run.

Forget getting unleashed. It's not worth it. This is too hard. It *feels* insurmountable because at this point in the process, you're hit with the weight of an undeniable truth:

Every problem starts as a leadership issue.

And you're a leader.

You followed the flames of your leadership problems. You thought you knew where those paths would lead. When you started digging, you thought you knew what you'd unearth. You wanted the smoldering source to blow cursive smoke of others' names. Hiss out stories of others' hidden mistakes. Instead, a tongue of fire licked toward you, and you backed away. All was revealed. You recognize this flame.

You helped strike the match.

We know what you're feeling right now. We've been there.

This is why many leaders will give up at this point. The weight of responsibility is heavy.

Imagine how Tamara must have felt when Sue lingered on that hefty "but" then said, "You esteem excellence so highly that efficiency is sacrificed." Tamara knew that "but" would be followed by a "you." That was the moment her hidden flame jumped up and licked her in the face. That never feels good.

But here is the good news: If every problem starts as a leadership issue, every solution starts with the leader. And that's you.

10

Determine Your Critical Actions

ONCE YOU KNOW the issues you're dealing with, you can turn them into traits that transform your leadership. Converting the issues into traits begins to tear away the fibers that have kept you leashed. The issue that once held you back will become the trait that sets you free. Now, you can move on to the third and final step of the Discern Stage: determine your critical actions. In this step, you will construct a handful of actions that will unleash you.

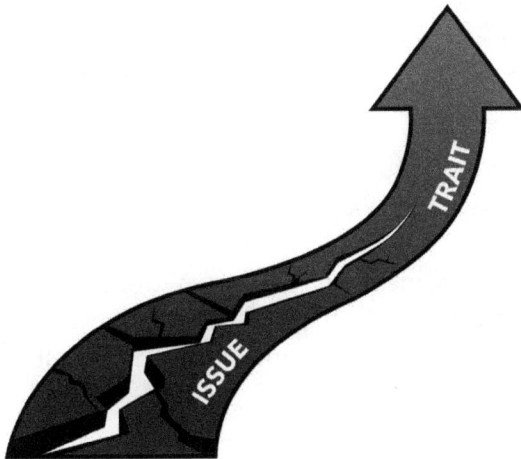

The 7 Traits of an Unleashed Leader[IP]

1. **Character:** Leaders demonstrate humility, take responsibility, and handle the uncomfortable challenges they used to avoid.
2. **Competence:** Leaders develop self-knowledge and the specific skills needed to guide the people and organization toward a better future.
3. **Capacity:** Leaders get better and faster results by increasing their reservoirs of time, energy, attention, and resources.
4. **Clarity:** Leaders keep everyone focused on where the organization is going, how it's getting there, and each person's role in getting there.
5. **Community:** Leaders provide a sense of safety, build trust throughout the team, and encourage collaboration.
6. **Culture:** Leaders shape the habits, attitudes, and behaviors so they align with the company's values.
7. **Consistency:** Leaders create a sense of stability, ensuring that everyone knows what to expect and what's expected of them.

Tamara's team helped her discover that Clarity and Consistency were the underlying issues of her presenting problems. Like Tamara, you may have more than one root issue on your hands. When this is the case, always move through the seven issues in order: Character, Competence, Capacity, Clarity, Community, Culture, and Consistency. Tamara needed to develop Clarity and supplement it with Consistency.

Three Steps to Determine Your Critical Actions

If you're like most leaders we know, you're busy. You don't need to add hundreds of additional activities to your task list. That would only keep you leashed. Instead, you need to generate a sprinkling of calculated actions to propel you forward. These three steps to determine your critical actions will only take a few minutes.

#1: Brainstorm actions that *could* help you develop the traits you need.

Grab a sheet of paper or open a document, and set a timer for five minutes. During that time, capture every possible action you can think of that could help you develop that trait.

- What *habits* could you establish?
- What resources (books, podcasts, videos, conferences, etc.) might accelerate your growth in this area?
- Who could you ask to help you develop these traits?

#2: Identify what you need to stop doing.

Unleashing these traits might require you to stop doing certain activities in two areas:

1. *What habits need to stop?*
   Are there repeated behaviors that will prevent you from developing these traits?

2. *What responsibilities do you need to stop or delegate?*
   Developing this new trait will take time. Rather than trying to cram your growth into the barely-there

margins you have, give something away. Is there a weekly meeting that you don't need to attend? Do you have a responsibility that you could delegate to someone?

#3: Determine the most critical actions to take over the next quarter.

Unless your list is really small, you won't have time to complete everything that's on your list. Follow Pareto's Principle: select the 20 percent of actions that will generate 80 percent of the transformation.

Unleashed Leadership is Book One of an eight-part series. The subsequent books will each dive deep into the seven traits of Unleashed Leadership and the best practices for getting unleashed from each issue.

సౌఒ

In Tamara's case, she knew the source of her problems – Clarity and Consistency. Now, she could turn these issues into leadership traits to develop. She identified five critical actions to upgrade her Clarity and Consistency.

1. *Meet with Mr. Patel to agree on a company purpose, values, and priorities.*
2. *Communicate these to my team, as well as each person's individual role in achieving our goals.*
3. *Repeat the purpose, values, and priorities every week in the team meeting, so we can use them when we make decisions.*

4. *Create three recipe SOPs every week with instructions and pictures, and give them to the team before they start cooking.*

5. *Stop doing any recipe tweaks after 10:30 am (unless our negligence will cause customers to get sick).*

∽⊛∾

You'll know you're through the Discern Stage when you have your list in hand. You have put in the hard thinking work—now it's time to take action!

To help you accelerate your work through Stages 2 and 3, we've created The Unleashed Momentum Map[IP]. Download your free copy here.

Go to UnleashedLeadership.com or scan this QR code.

Stage 3: Deliver

03

DELIVER

☐ Activate your critical actions
(Chapter 11)

☐ Accelerate your unleashing
(Chapter 12)

WE (GARLAND AND Dorothy) have an unusual relationship. We were coworkers for an organization, then cofounders of our own. And, if you haven't picked up on it yet, before we were coworkers or cofounders, we were a couple.

On November 27, 1999, we stood in front of 200 loved ones and proclaimed vows to each other. We promised that we would love each other for better or worse, richer or poorer, in sickness and in health, as long as we both shall live.

Months before that day, we *decided* we wanted to spend our lives together. Then, we went through an engagement period, learning methods of dealing with the inevitable challenges of marriage during premarital counseling. We *discerned* plans for dealing with finances, emotions, priorities, conflict, children, etc.

Finally, we had a ceremony solidifying those first two stages and moving us into a third. Since that day in 1999, we have been *delivering* on our decision and discernment. Like any marriage, there have been seasons when delivery was easy. But there have also been seasons when delivery has been more challenging.

The first two stages of getting unleashed—Decide and Discern—don't take as long to do. The third stage, Deliver, is the shortest to explain but the longest to carry out. Why?

Transformation takes time.

Developing each of the Unleashed Leadership traits is like building muscle. If you want to grow your biceps, you can't do one workout and expect Arnold Schwarzenegger's arms. It takes focused effort over time to get results.

The same is true for upgrading leadership traits. It takes far less time to discover what's holding you back than it does to make progress.

11

Activate Your Critical Actions

IN THE DELIVER stage, you will create and execute a plan based on your critical actions, transforming your leadership issues into leadership traits. This stage usually takes 1–6 months, depending on two factors:

1. How much work you need to do to turn issues into traits.
2. How much concentrated effort you devote to growth.

You'll turn your critical action into an Unleashed Momentum Map (UMM). This set of daily, weekly, monthly, and quarterly rhythms will release the leash.

#1: Review your critical actions.

In Stage 2, you determined the critical actions that will turn your leadership issues into traits. You've already seen Tamara's critical actions:

1. *Meet with Mr. Patel to agree on a company purpose, values, and priorities. (Clarity)*
2. *Communicate these to my team, as well as each person's individual role in achieving our goals. (Clarity)*

3. *Repeat the purpose, values, and priorities every week in the team meeting so we can use them when we make decisions. (Clarity & Consistency)*
4. *Create three recipe SOPs every week with instructions and pictures and give to the team before they start cooking. (Clarity & Consistency)*
5. *Stop doing any recipe tweaks after 10:30 am (unless our negligence will cause customers to get sick). (Consistency)*

#2. Plan your action steps every week.

Each week, spend ten minutes looking over your critical actions. Establish the steps you need to take this week to make progress.

Each week may look different. For example, Tamara's first critical action was to meet with Mr. Patel. In the first week, she could schedule that meeting, but he might not be available until Week 3. After the meeting, he may require a couple of weeks to think about the purpose, values, and priorities. She might not receive his input until Week 5.

This would delay critical actions 2 and 3. However, she can move forward with critical actions 4 and 5 by getting started with her recipe SOPs and stopping any recipe tweaks after 10:30 am.

Write these steps down in your Unleashed Action Tracker^{IP}. This tool will help you keep up with all the steps you need to complete each week to make progress.

You'll find the Unleashed Action Tracker in the Unleashed Momentum Map, which you can access for free using the QR code at the end of this chapter.

#3: Review your tasks daily.

Every day, take one minute to review your Unleashed Action Tracker for the week. Identify any tasks you need to complete today. This habit will keep these actions on your mind and in your calendar.

#4: Reflect weekly.

At the end of each week, take 10 minutes to review the progress you've made on your actions. Start by determining the percentage of your steps that you accomplished this week. Aim for no less than 85 percent completion every week.[9]

Next, answer three questions:

1. What did I accomplish that helped me grow as a leader this week?
2. What am I grateful for as a leader this week?
3. What will I do differently next week to make me a better leader?[10]

You can record all of these insights in the Scorecard section of your Unleashed Momentum Map.

#5: Solicit feedback monthly.

Get your supervisor, peers, and team involved in your unleashing. They will be the direct beneficiaries of your work. Share with them how you're striving to grow and the actions that you

---

[9] Brian Moran and Michael Lennington say this: "We have found that if you successfully complete 85% of the activities in your weekly plan, then you will most likely achieve your objectives." *The 12 Week Year: Get More Done in 12 Weeks than Others Do in 12 Months.* Hoboken, John Wiley & Sons, 2013.

[10] I (Garland) share more about these questions in *Gettin' (un)Busy: 5 Steps to Kill Busyness and Live with Purpose, Productivity, and Peace.* During my doctoral research, I found that these three questions helps leaders reflect each week and become more productive without increasing their stress.

plan on taking this week. Invite them to encourage you, raise questions, and hold you accountable.

Once a month, ask several of them what progress they've seen and where you're still stuck. By including them, you demonstrate that you value their feedback and trust them to support you in your leadership journey.

#6: Renew or rewrite your critical actions every quarter.

At the end of each three-month focus, return to Stage 2, Discern.

- What are your current presenting problems?
- What underlying leadership issue(s) do these problems indicate?
- What leadership trait(s) do you need to develop in the next three months?

If you still need to work on the same issue(s), recommit and re-discern what needs to happen. If a fresh challenge has arisen, discern a new plan and start delivering.

Leadership is a lifelong journey. No one has ever fully arrived. You will always have areas to unleash. Reactivating a UMM every quarter will help you avoid the tug of the leash.

To help you accelerate your work through Stages 2 and 3, we've created The Unleashed Momentum Map. Download your free copy here.

Go to UnleashedLeadership.com or scan this QR code.

12

Accelerate Your Unleashing

UNLEASHED LEADERSHIP IS Book One of an eight-part series. The subsequent books will each dive deep into the seven traits of Unleashed Leadership and the best practices (we call these Breakaways) of getting unleashed from each issue. Even if you are planning to read the rest of the series, you probably want help right now. No matter which trait you're working on, we offer resources to accelerate your unleashing.

1. Subscribe and Search Friday 411.

Friday 411 is our weekly leadership newsletter. Every Friday, we send out a newsletter that you can read in less than four (4) minutes, and it contains one (1) leadership insight and gives you one (1) action to take based on that insight. You can subscribe for free at AdVanceLeadership.live/blog.

Additionally, you can search through previous articles to find guidance on specific traits you want to develop. You can find these at AdVanceLeadership.live/blog.

2. Find a mentor.

A good mentor can help you avoid common mistakes, learn more quickly, and see your blind spots. If you know someone who already has a trait you want, ask them to mentor you for a couple of months. Tell them how you see the trait in them, and ask them to help you develop it.

Finding mentors is one of the quickest ways to accelerate your growth. If you want help making the most of a mentoring relationship, download our free guide, How to Make the Most of a Mentoring Relationship, at UnleashedLeadership.com.

3. Hire an Unleashed Leadership Executive Coach.

Executive Coaching is a proven and effective way to accelerate your growth as a leader. You may be seeking individual support, or you may be an HR Leader who needs coaching for multiple employees. Either way, by using proprietary tools, an Unleashed Leadership Executive Coach can help navigate all three stages.

To find out more, email us at coaching@advanceleadership.live.

〜✿〜

So far, these resources have focused on you as a solitary leader. But we believe that good leaders become great when they're surrounded by other unleashed leaders. In 2018, the Center for Creative Leadership found that 76 percent of executives experienced feelings of loneliness. Of those surveyed, 58 percent believed it negatively affected their decision-making abilities.[11]

The loneliness of leadership is a common experience, but it doesn't have to be that way. The remainder of the resources will help you connect with other leaders who are hungry to positively impact their teams and organizations.

4. Start an Unleashed Leadership Group.

Pick a few other leaders you admire and invite them to become part of an Unleashed Leadership Group. After everyone completes this book, meet every 1–2 weeks to share your progress, discuss current challenges, and advise each other.

For insights on how to lead the first few sessions of an Unleashed Leadership Group, download the free guide at UnleashedLeadership.com.

---

[11] "How Loneliness Is Shaping the Future of Leadership: Hello Coach," Hello Coach, April 23, 2025, https://hello-coach.com/blog/how-loneliness-is-shaping-the-future-of-leadership.

5. Join the Unleashed Community.

We host an online community of leaders from multiple industries and levels of leadership—united by one goal: to unleash their leadership and multiply their impact. This is where you'll find the encouragement, fresh insight, and practical tools you need to overcome challenges and align your team. We use a mix of training sessions, Q&A, peer coaching, and mini workshops.

If you join this community:

- **You'll never lead alone again.**
  Surround yourself with trusted peers who understand the weight you carry and will stand with you through every win and challenge.

- **You'll turn vision into results.**
  Get the tools, strategies, and support you need to align your team, create momentum, and accomplish your most important goals.

- **You'll lead with confidence, not chaos.**
  Escape the pull of constant demands and relentless pressure. Learn to focus on what matters most, manage your energy, and lead from strength instead of stress.

- **You'll get unleashed.**
  Complex challenges don't have to keep you stuck. We'll help you apply the seven traits of Unleashed Leadership so you can solve problems faster and lead with purpose.

Visit AdVanceLeadership.live/joincommunity to
connect with your unleashed community.

6. Lead a Transformation.

If you're in HR, Learning & Development, or a C-Suite Leader,
you can unleash leaders at scale throughout your organization.
Transformations are multi-month training programs that help
leaders at every level get unleashed.

We'll help you identify your company's biggest leadership
issues and create a customized program. We only lead a few of
these transformations every year, so email us at transform@
advanceleadership.live to find out more information and schedule a time to see if your organization is a right fit.

Conclusion

WE DON'T KNOW about you, but we hate books that make grandiose guarantees. You know, the ones that claim if you follow their exact methods, you will solve *all your problems and never struggle again.* Too many people overpromise and underdeliver so you'll buy whatever they're selling. We don't want to do that to you.

Here is our promise: *you will continue to face challenges.* Every leader endures countless problems, crises, and difficult situations. Each new stage of your growth will deliver disparity between your responsibilities and abilities. As long as you are in leadership, you will have times when you feel that leash.

Our process is not designed to resolve all your issues all at once. The remaining books in *The Unleashed Leadership Series* will serve as ridiculously practical guides for how to get unleashed from each issue. (We originally planned to put them all in one book, but that book would have been over 1,000 pages. When was the last time you read a 1,000-page book? It's been *never* for us.)

Instead, this first book provides a three-stage framework to help you discern the root leadership issues that hold you back and accelerate your ability to get unleashed. They unleash your team to greater productivity and your company to better results. Those three stages are:

1. **Decide** that you will get unleashed.
2. **Discern** what got you leashed and how to get unleashed.
3. **Deliver** the actions that will get you unleashed.

That's exactly what Larry did. (Remember Larry? You met him in the Introduction.)

⚬⚬⚬

At 1:27 a.m., Larry sat alone in his home office, staring blankly at the list on his notepad, each task another stone added to the already crushing weight. He dropped his head into his hands and whispered the words he had been thinking for months:

"I am a bad leader."

Despair flooded him. He felt embarrassed, defeated, and exhausted. He thought about his team—how they seemed lost and frustrated. His mind wandered to Carter, his boss, who expected progress that Larry couldn't deliver. Sighing, he envisioned his wife and kids, who barely got the leftovers of the man they loved. He was failing them all.

That belief could have haunted Larry for the rest of his career. It could have destroyed his confidence and led to terrible decisions and poor treatment of people. But when he said the words out loud, they didn't sound quite right. Larry knew his past successes proved he was not a *bad* leader. He was something else.

Again, he spoke out loud: "I am *not* a bad leader. I'm just stuck. I feel…"

The word escaped him. Held back? Choked? He put his hands to his throat, where he felt an invisible tightening. And then it came to him.

I feel leashed.

It was then that he heard footsteps in the hallway. His office door creaked open. His wife stood on the threshold, her tousled bedhead illuminated by the dim light of the moon through the window.

"Hey," she said empathetically. "Can't sleep?"

"Yeah," Larry admitted. "You still having trouble sleeping, too?"

"Actually," she walked over to him and sat across his lap, wrapping an arm around his shoulders and laying her temple against his forehead. "I've been sleeping a lot better lately."

"I'm so glad to hear that. What changed?"

"I got unleashed."

Larry startled at the word. "*Un*leashed?"

"Yeah. You know how badly I was struggling with keeping customers, not knowing how to turn things around. I felt like such a failure as a leader. But then I realized I wasn't broken. I was bound."

His wife's insight ignited a spark. For the first time in weeks, Larry felt a flicker of hope.

He shifted his weight to look his wife in the eyes, placing a hand on her face. "Tamara, how did you get unleashed?"

She smiled. "I was hoping you'd ask."

Tamara reached across and pulled her own notepad out of a desk drawer. Larry noticed the words Unleashed Leadership across the top and his wife's familiar scribbling down the rest of the page. She flipped back a few pages and pointed to her notes.

"Let me introduce you to the seven issues that keep you leashed and the three stages to get unleashed."

That night, Larry made a decision that would change everything: he would not stay stuck. Like his wife, Tamara, he would get unleashed. He completed **Stage 1: Decide.**

The next morning, Larry started **Stage 2: Discern.** He began by naming all his presenting problems.

With pen and paper, he poured out all the frustrations and challenges he had been carrying.

Endless emails

Constant interruptions

Late nights

No matter how hard I work, it's never enough

Frustrated team members

Overflowing calendar

Everyone needs me for every decision

Missed baseball games

Missed metrics

Lack of clear priorities

Being accused of being unavailable and directionless

He felt tempted to blame all of this on the CEO... or Carter... or the culture at his company... or his predecessor. But he knew that blaming others feels great in the moment but inhibits any power to change.

Even as he wrote them all down, Larry could see the truth: All of these grievances were symptoms, not the root issue. They were the smoke, not the fire.

Larry's list led him to the second step of the **Discern Stage: Identifying the Underlying Leadership Issue(s).** After working through the Unleashed Leadership framework, Larry discovered that he had three issues:

1. **Capacity:** He didn't have the time, energy, and attention to lead effectively.
2. **Clarity:** He could not see or communicate the vision of where his team was going or how to get there.
3. **Community:** He did not trust the members of his team to make decisions without him, and they knew it.

Larry knew that he needed to deal with **Capacity** first. If he started anywhere else, he would only add more responsibilities to his overflowing plate. He recognized that his greatest assets were his hard work, long hours, and "everything is figure-outable" attitude. His old methods for managing time, energy, and attention no longer worked in this role. If he didn't change, he wasn't just risking his own career. He was risking the success of every person who depended on him, as well as their well-being and happiness.

> Blaming others feels great in the moment but inhibits any power to change.

He completed the third step of the **Discern Stage: Identifying the Underlying Leadership Issue(s),** in 30 minutes.

Larry built a simple but clear plan to upgrade his Capacity. Here's what he landed on.

1. Take 10 minutes every day to prioritize what I must do. Limit it to three items.
2. Block time every day for conversations with team members to hear about their obstacles and insights.
3. Learn to use an AI tool that tames my unruly inbox and helps me identify my most important emails.
4. Put away my phone and laptop from 6:00–8:00 p.m. every night. I will only pull them out if Tamara and I agree that I absolutely must.
5. Delegate at least 5 responsibilities every week to free my brain to think about bigger decisions.
6. Talk openly with my team, peers, and Carter about my capacity challenges, the problems I'm causing, and my plan for unleashing my leadership.

Creating a plan provided Larry with some immediate relief. The leash loosened, and he could breathe a little easier.

As Larry delivered on his plan, the panic and shame he had once felt started to lift. Evenings with his family became lighter. His team grew more capable. His energy returned. Within two months, Larry had freed up significant amounts of time, energy, and attention.

With fresh breathing room, Larry could look again at his leadership and his team. He realized that the team expended tremendous effort but made minimal progress. Because they weren't clear on their highest priorities, they viewed everything as equally important. His team's unawareness of the goals meant that *he had leashed them* through his lack of **Clarity**.

Larry recounted the conversation he had with Carter a few months prior. He had asked Carter which of the 20 metrics were the three most important. Carter replied, "The three most important are all of them."

It occurred to Larry that the whole organization struggled with **Clarity**. He couldn't fix the whole company, but he could upgrade his own leadership.

Larry followed the three stages again.

- He **decided** to get unleashed.
- He **discerned** the presenting problems, leadership issues, and traits to upgrade.
- He took action to **deliver** on that plan.

Here's Larry's plan to unleash his **Clarity**.

1. Work with Carter to choose the three most important goals for my team in the next six months.
2. Assign leaders to each goal and have them build small teams around them.
3. Establish a meeting rhythm for the whole team to align on goals, responsibilities, and clear plans.
4. Document all standard Operating Procedures for repeatable work to cut down confusion and speed up execution.
5. Publicly post goals and updates so everyone can see and celebrate them.
6. Review and update Carter monthly on progress and obstacles regarding the goals.

Momentum exploded. Larry's department hit new performance levels, and other departments noticed. The CEO noticed. When he saw the results of Larry's team's efforts, he realized the **Clarity** issue was company-wide. He asked Larry to show him the Unleashed Leadership framework so that he could learn to build **Clarity** throughout the organization.

After implementing his **Capacity** and **Clarity** upgrades, Larry's team grew more confident and capable, but they weren't yet cohesive.

Larry looked at the presenting problems and remembered that it was a **Community** issue that led to his first employee quitting. He realized that he didn't know the people on the team very well, and that many of them struggled to trust him and each other. He saw problems like ineffective collaboration and a lot of arguing. Larry knew that it was time to unleash his Community. Again, he Decided, Discerned, and Delivered.

Here is Larry's plan to unleash his **Community**.

1. Pursue each team member individually to develop a relationship where I get to know them personally and professionally.
2. Host an off-site planning retreat that includes time for each individual to share about their lives.
3. Allow 10 minutes at the beginning of our team's weekly meeting for casual conversation.
4. Collaborate with the team to create a set of principles that govern how we treat each other, work together, and make decisions.
5. Build trust by supporting my team members' decisions, encouraging them when they fail, and celebrating them when they succeed.

It took another few months for Larry to deliver on this plan, but these small changes made a huge difference. During the company's annual employee survey, Larry's team had the highest rate of satisfaction and the lowest turnover.

Every few months, Larry would pause, reexamine his leadership, and ask: *Where am I currently leashed?* Sometimes it was a *self-development issue*, like avoiding hard conversations.

Sometimes it was a *team development issue*, like letting bad behavior linger too long.

But he no longer saw these moments as proof he was failing. They served as a sign it was time to Decide, Discern, and Deliver.

❧

Now, it's your turn to Decide, Discern, and Deliver.
But not just for your own sake.
Your team, company, family, and the world need you.
It's time to unleash your leadership.

Your leadership matters. You've got this,

Garland & Dorothy

Garland's Thanks

THE BEST PARTS of my story are the people I get to share it with.

Dorothy—We have collaborated in so many ways for over 25 years—in building a home, a family, ministries, a business, and writing. Every collaboration becomes better and more fun when you get involved. It is the greatest privilege of my life to venture together with you.

Calvin, Sophie, and Toby—I am so grateful to call you my kids and believe you are called and equipped to make the world better for every person you encounter. Calvin—You inspire me with your resilience and optimism, even in hard times. Sophie—I am overjoyed by your hard work and drive for excellence. Toby—I adore your joy of learning and your kindness to others. Thank you all for the gift of calling you my kiddos.

Dad and Mom—As a young man, you told me that I was a leader, and I always rolled my eyes. But you planted a grain of sand in my mind that became a pearl. Thank you for seeing what I could not.

Tim and Shirley—You welcomed me as your son long before it was official. Thank you for your constant encouragement, support, and belief.

Gordon, Lisa, John & Little Shirley—Thank you all for your quiet faithfulness and active support. You have been there for the most challenging seasons of life.

Justin Raby—Our miles of bike rides help me think more clearly, and your friendship has challenged me to live intentionally for the last 30 years.

Ben Miller—With friendship, keen insights, and fresh perspectives, you push me to think more deeply and creatively.

John Moore—You are the brother I never had and the one I always wanted. I can always count on your listening ears, praying heart, wise insights, and contagious enthusiasm.

Quinton Misenheimer—I will never forget your support professionally and personally in some of the most challenging moments of my life.

Mike McKenzie and Michael White—You were the first two to embrace and support *Unleashed Leadership*. Thank you both for entrusting me with the sacred task of developing the leaders under your care.

To the many friends who have allowed me to share ideas, geek out over hats, or discuss the challenges of leadership: Josh and Amber Hembree; Brent Williams; Cory Stuart; John and Amber Roberts; Brad McDonald and Jonathan Darling (thanks for unleashing leaders alongside us); Justin Clark; Rob Jeppsen; our small group friends who have prayed for our lives and this book series; and so many wonderful LinkedIn connections who leave comments, ask questions, and engage in conversations offline.

Dorothy's Thanks

MY CONTRIBUTIONS IN shaping *Unleashed Leadership* are not the ideas of an isolated individual but rather the sum of all who have influenced me. I am overwhelmed with gratitude for all the people who have molded my thoughts, beliefs, and actions throughout my life.

Whenever I want to give someone my highest compliment, I tell them *they're the type of person it feels like a privilege to know.* Over the years, I have been fortunate to have collected a great number of relationships with people who I am privileged to know.

Family is precious to me, a kindredship that runs deep. Woods, Tates, Barnetts, McGehees/Dickinsons, Skeltons/Whitleys, Foxes, Pattersons—to be in your presence feels like coming home. I hope you see the heart of our family's legacy beating throughout the values reflected in these pages. It's a privilege to be one of you and share these great names.

To all the people in Gainesville, FL, who helped raise me: Tim and Diane Adams—I was lucky enough to have you as a set of "bonus" parents. I miss you, Coach. Jane Williams—You showed me how essential it is to always have women in leadership. I hold you up as a model of what it looks like to lead and love people well. Ed Stefansen—You were like an encouraging big brother, calling out strengths in me that I didn't see in myself. Mary Drummond—You have always exhibited the kind of fearlessness I aspire toward. I am privileged to have come from such a strong foundation of leadership.

Some of the greatest privileges of my life have been found in friendships. My college "Girls," Steph, Stace, Becky, Brooke, and Jenn: thank you for navigating life's joys and sorrows together for over 30 years. To my friends in Rome, GA: thank you for taking me in at my most broken and showing me what true friendship looks like. To my friends in Katy, TX: I was only with you for two years but experienced some of the most remarkable and sweetest friendships I have known. And to my friends in Knoxville, TN: Amy Stuart—What a providential gift your friendship has been. I'm so thankful that your family moved in across the street the same month we arrived. Earl's small group—It's a joy to share life with you and have your unyielding support. The ladies of the Second Tuesday Book Club—I marvel at all of you—whip-smart, fierce, resilient. Any time I have with any of you, my friends, is a privilege.

And now to my greatest privileges:

My children's Granna and Poppa—I am forever grateful for all the years you devoted to intentionally breaking generational strongholds and raising my husband into the man he would become. Thank you also for adoring my babies. I miss you, Katherine. It is a privilege to be your daughter-in-love.

Gordon—Your words may be few, but each one is weighted in wisdom, humor, or both. You have given me incredible gifts: 1) My beloved sister-in-law, Lisa, niece, Shirley, and nephew, John, and 2) you have been there when I needed you most. It is a privilege to be your sister.

Mom and Dad—Some people luck out with a great mother. Some with a great father. What did I do to deserve both? I have spent my life witnessing all the people who flock toward you because of how you treat them—with honor, dignity, and respect. Thank you for shaping my views of exceptional leadership—that it cannot be separated from loving others well. It is a privilege to be your daughter.

My children—We chose your names so that their meanings would help guide your lives. Now that you all are moving into young adulthood, we are overjoyed to see you embody the qualities we hoped for you. Calvin—"Bold, strong, and powerful." You have displayed more courage and perseverance in your two decades than I have in my five. Sophia—"Wisdom." I could not be prouder of the level-headed, intelligent, diligent, creative woman we are sending out into the world. Tobiah—"The Lord is good." Your dynamic curiosity, empathy, and loving-kindness point to the goodness of God. Instead of dwelling on the sacrifice it takes to have a mom who writes and travels, the three of you have chosen to become my biggest cheerleaders. I would not be able to do what I do without that gift. It is an incredible privilege to be your mom.

My husband—It has been said that the test of true character is whether or not a person practices at home what he preaches in public. If that is the case, I can attest that you embody every bit of what you teach. You are a man who lives with intention and enthusiasm and loves others deeply and authentically. I stand in awe of your brilliance, secured in your loyalty, and bolstered by your support. Every day, there is at least one moment when I recognize that being your wife is the greatest privilege of my life.

Our Thanks

THOSE WHO HAVE walked beside us have helped shape the pages of this book.

Brittni Wareham—Thank you for managing the chaos that we throw at you every week. Your joy and laughter make life better, and you skillfully handle the areas that we are so ill-equipped to do.

The Igniting Souls team—Kary, Sarah, Teri, Debbie, Jill, Jillian, Tanisha, and Melissa—Thanks for believing in our vision of creating this series of books, for enabling us to turn them into reality, and for helping us get unstuck whenever we mired ourselves down.

Jeremy Floyd—Thank you for using your impressive gifts to mobilize us and help us see what we couldn't.

To all those who read, reviewed, critiqued, edited, and supported *Unleashed Leadership*— Thank you for your wisdom and feedback. Our names may be on the cover, but your insights made this book better.

To our clients across the world—Thank you for being leaders who *want* to grow so that you can benefit the people you lead and the customers you serve. Every person deserves to have a great leader, and we're grateful for the energy and effort you each put into that calling. When we're with you, our favorite moments are when we shut up and listen and let you all do the talking. Spending time around so many outstanding leaders, we learn more than we teach.

There are some people who have become more than clients. They are colleagues and friends:

Scott Ferguson—Thank you for demonstrating that you get better results when you put people first. We are grateful to call you and Dee our friends.

Silvia Costa—You add enthusiasm and energy to everyone you touch. Anyone who finds themselves under your leadership is lucky to be there.

Jeff Smith—Thank you for letting us partner with you in two of your ventures. We hold you up as one of the greats—a leader others should emulate. You make people and organizations better, and we're blessed to know you. Your leadership inspires us to build even more leaders.

The entire Rollins corporation—We're so grateful for our years of partnership. You are creating a special and spectacular company. Thank you for letting us in on the secret—that the pest control industry attracts the kindest, most gracious people out there.

Jamie Benton—Thank you for your passion to develop leaders at every level.

Gelair Butler—You know you've been in Garland's Top 5 for years. Now that Dorothy has gotten to know you, you've inevitably made her list, too.

Jackie Westmoreland, Clarissa Mitchell, Hayden Holmes, and Mavis Chiwandire—It's a joy to partner together to build a leadership culture.

Pat Chrzanowski and Stanford Phillips—Thank you for modeling and guiding everyone toward heroic impact, essential together, and being remarkable.

Jerry Gahlhoff—You set the standard for building a company that intentionally develops leaders. You have cheered on many leaders, including us, for so many years. The world is a better place because of your visionary, servant-hearted leadership.

All the RMDP participants over the years—Knowing each of you is one of the great joys of our lives. Your leadership matters.

Whether at home or traveling, we love to support local coffee shops however we can. A special thank you to all those where we set up shop to write. In Knoxville—Potchke Bagel, Honeybee, K Brew. Local coffee shops in NYC, DC, Atlanta, Toronto, Montreal, Calgary, Lodi, LA, Phoenix, Dallas, Orlando, Philadelphia, St. Louis—Thank you for hosting us.

Finally, to you who have used your valuable time to read this book—Thank you for being the kind of leader who cares about results and relationships and the kind of person who wants to enhance the lives of those you lead. The world needs more leaders like you.

About the Authors

Dr. Garland Vance believes every person deserves to work with a great leader and every leader can be great. He has spent over 25 years helping organizations develop the leaders they need to succeed. With his wife, Dorothy, he cofounded AdVance Leadership, which helps companies develop the leaders they need to succeed.

After earning his doctorate in Leadership and Spiritual Formation, he authored *Gettin' (un)Busy*, which *Forbes* named "one of the seven books everyone on your team should read" and 2020's Best Business Book by Author Academy Awards.

He is also an avid collector of baseball caps with weird logos. He lives in Knoxville, Tennessee, with Dorothy, their three kids, a turtle, and a lovebird.

He writes about Unleashed Leadership regularly at

AdVanceLeadership.live/blog and on LinkedIn
at LinkedIn.com/in/garland-vance.

Dorothy Wood Vance has been helping leaders discover and maximize their unique talents and gifts for over 25 years, empowering good leaders to become great. With her husband, Garland, she cofounded AdVance Leadership, which is recognized as one of the Top 20 Leadership Development Companies in America.

She and Garland live with their three children in Knoxville, Tennessee. In her spare time, you'll usually find her somewhere outdoors–from hiking a trail through the mountains to her back porch with a good book.

She regularly writes about Unleashed Leadership at

AdVanceLeadership.live/blog.

Discover Ridiculously Practical Insights to Unleash Your Leadership

Friday 411
NEWSLETTER

- Delivered to your inbox every Friday
- Takes 4 minutes or less to read
- Provides 1 insight to unleash your leadership
- Gives 1 practical action for you to take in the next week

THIS BOOK IS PROTECTED INTELLECTUAL PROPERTY

Instant IP [IP]

The author of this book values Intellectual Property. The book you just read is protected by Instant IP[IP], a proprietary process, which integrates blockchain technology giving Intellectual Property "Global Protection." By creating a "Time-Stamped" smart contract that can never be tampered with or changed, we establish "First Use" that tracks back to the author.

Instant IP [IP] functions much like a Pre-Patent since it provides an immutable "First Use" of the Intellectual Property. This is achieved through our proprietary process of leveraging blockchain technology and smart contracts. As a result, proving "First Use" is simple through a global and verifiable smart contract. By protecting intellectual property with blockchain technology and smart contracts, we establish a "First to File" event.

Protected by Instant IP [IP]

LEARN MORE AT INSTANTIP.TODAY

www.ingramcontent.com/pod-product-compliance
Lightning Source LLC
Chambersburg PA
CBHW071426210326
41597CB00020B/3674